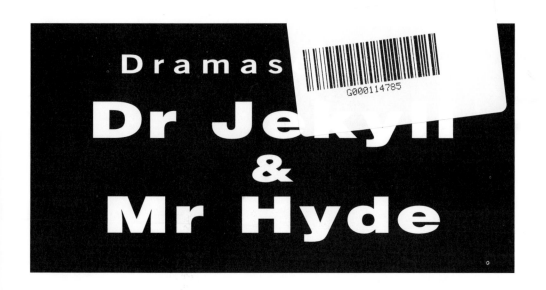

Dramas

Dr Jekyll & Mr Hyde

ROBERT LOUIS STEVENSON

Dramatised by
DAVID CALCUTT

Nelson

Thomas Nelson & Sons Ltd
Nelson House
Mayfield Road
Walton-on-Thames
Surrey KT12 5PL
United Kingdom

Dr Jekyll and Mr Hyde – the script © David Calcutt 1999
The right of David Calcutt to be identified as the author of this play has been asserted by David Calcutt in accordance with the Copyright, Design and Patents Act 1988.
All applications to perform this play should be addressed in the first instance to the Royalty and Permissions Department, ITPS Ltd, Cheriton House, North Way, Andover, Hampshire SP10 5BE (*Telephone* 01264 342756; *Fax* 01264 342792).

Introduction, activities and explanatory notes
© Thomas Nelson 1999

Edited by Liz Harman
Designed and produced by Bender Richardson White
Typesetting by Malcolm Smythe
Cover illustration by Dave Grimwood
Black and white illustrations by John James
Printed by Zrinski Printing and Publishing House, Čakovec, Croatia

This edition published by Thomas Nelson & Sons Ltd 1999
ISBN 0–17 432599–1
9 8 7 6 5 4 3 2
03   02   01   00   99

CONTENTS

SERIES EDITOR'S INTRODUCTION

Dramascripts is an exciting series of plays especially chosen for students in the lower and middle years of secondary school. The titles range from the best in modern writing to adaptations of classic texts such as *A Christmas Carol* and *Silas Marner*.

Dramascripts can be read or acted purely for the enjoyment and stimulation that they provide; however, each play in the series also offers all the support that pupils need in working with the text in the classroom:

- **Introduction** – this offers important background information and explains something about the ways in which the play came to be written.
- **Script** – this is clearly set out in ways that make the play easy to handle in the classroom.
- **Notes** explain references that pupils might not understand, and language points that are not obvious.
- **Activities** – at the end of scenes, acts or sections – give pupils the opportunity to explore the play more fully. Types of activity include: discussion, writing, hot-seating, improvisation, acting, freeze-framing, story-boarding and artwork.
- **Looking Back at the Play** – this section has further activities for more extended work on the play as a whole with emphasis on characters, plots, themes and language.

INTRODUCTION

Dr Jekyll and Mr Hyde by Robert Louis Stevenson is perhaps one of the most original and influential stories written in English. It has entered popular mythology, through several films and stage adaptations, and its title has become a part of the English language itself – someone who appears to have two distinct sides to their personality is often described as a 'Jekyll and Hyde' character. And this popularity has not been slowly acquired – the book achieved immediate popularity upon its publication in 1885, and brought Stevenson, at last, the recognition and fame he desired.

Writing a new adaptation of such a work presents many problems. Perhaps the chief of these is the knowledge that there have been many previous fine adaptations, which can prompt the desire to 'do something different', if only for the sake of being different. That in itself is not really a good enough reason, but when I came to read Stevenson's story again, I realised that, in order to make a new adaptation, I would indeed have to 'do something different'.

The first thing I wanted to do was to get away from the idea that the transformation scenes – where Jekyll becomes Hyde, and vice-versa – should involve the actor 'disappearing' behind a settee or a cupboard and, after a few strangulated gargles, re-appear wearing a mask. That seemed to be too comical for what I saw as an essentially serious, and in many ways, disturbing event. So I decided to have Jekyll and Hyde played by two separate actors. This would not only avoid any disappearing act, but would also emphasise the idea that Hyde, while being an aspect of

Jekyll, is also a completely separate being – a being, in fact, much stronger and more powerful than Jekyll.

But I soon realised that, in order to create a piece of theatre, I was going to have to expand upon, or even create new scenes out of, the events of the story. For Stevenson's novella is a model of subtle storytelling. The tale is not told in anything like a straightforward manner, is full of hints and guesswork, with events being partially narrated by different characters, and it's only in the final pages that we at last are presented with the 'truth' as to the horror that's been happening. In a sense, it works a little like a detective story, with the reader in the role of detective, trying to work out, from the clues that are given what's going on. Realising that gave me the idea for creating an actual detective for the play, someone who, on our behalf, would investigate 'the strange case of Dr Jekyll and Mr Hyde', and, through the collection of evidence, gradually build the story for us.

And what evidence was he to collect? Here again, I found myself having to open out the story, develop characters and incidents sketched briefly in the original story, and even invent some of my own. But, in this, I like to think I was always true to the spirit of Stevenson. Some incidents could be taken from his story and developed. Others, the invented ones, I took from other works by Stevenson, and even from his own life. For I knew that *Dr Jekyll and Mr Hyde* had its origin in a dream (Stevenson was prone to such vivid dreams) and that its theme was close to him – how we carry within us more than one personality, a secret that is often savage and dangerous. In Stevenson's time this idea itself was dangerous, and shocking. I think he was the first writer to properly explore it. To us, it may seem more commonplace, and an accepted truism. But that doesn't make it any less true – or any less disturbing.

This adaptation, then, is not strictly Stevenson's novella as written. It's more like a collaboration between Stevenson and myself. And I like to think that, with his help, I've managed to create a play that is, if nothing else, in his own words, 'a real crawler'.

The play has not been divided into acts and it is intended that it should be performed with each scene flowing seamlessly on from the one before. To this end, minimal scenery will be required.

David Calcutt

THE CHARACTERS

DR HENRY JEKYLL *A doctor.*

EDWARD HYDE *His alter-ego.*

MR UTTERSON *A lawyer, a friend of Dr Jekyll.*

SERGEANT KINCH *A private detective.*

RICHARD ENFIELD *A 'man about town'.*

MR EDWARD LANYON *A surgeon.*

SIR DANVERS CAREW *A politician.*

LADY CAREW *His wife.*

YOUNG JEKYLL *Henry Jekyll at the age of 12.*

JANET *His nanny.*

MARY *A prostitute.*

LINK BOY *Aged about 14.*

BEDLAMITE

WARDER

LAZARUS *A grave-robber.*

MARTHA *A grave-robber.*

CRONE *An old woman.*

THE DAMNED of the city – *Crone, Link boy, Resurrection man, Resurrection woman, Bedlamite and Harlot (Mary could play the Harlot, Lazarus and Martha the Resurrection man and woman, Tommy the Link boy; the Bedlamite and Crone can be the same in all scenes).*

DR JEKYLL AND MR HYDE
SCENE 1

The street where Jekyll lives

The stage is dimly lit. JEKYLL enters, and speaks to the audience.

JEKYLL	I have walked the winding streets of the dark city. I have followed the course of my footsteps where no light shines, and where love is unknown. Shadows without faces have passed by me in the darkness, formless, melting into the fog of the night. And I have stood before closed doorways in dank alleys, with trembling hands and an eager heart, and heard the voices that cry from within – the drunkard's howl, the beggar's laugh, the harlot's groan – all the cursed and cursing voices of the damned.	1
		10

(From within the doorways along the street, we hear the voices of THE DAMNED of the city call out.)

CRONE   Just give me some of mother's ruin!

LINK BOY   Light your way, sir?

RESURRECTION MAN   A little of what you fancy does you good!

HARLOT   Looking for a good time, are you, dearie?

harlot *Prostitute.*

crone *Withered old woman.*

mother's ruin *Gin.*

Link boy At the time the play is set, many streets had no lighting. Some poor children earned a little money lighting people's way through the dark, often dangerous streets. A 'link' was a piece of wood dipped in pitch (a substance that burns well) and lit.

RESURRECTION WOMAN	Where's the money! Give me the blasted money!
BEDLAMITE	Hold him down! Keep him still while I finish the job!
JEKYLL	Crying in fear, crying in pain, crying in the terrible joy of their damnation. I have heard them – and sought to join them.
	(A central door swings open. The figure of HYDE stands there. He is lit directly from behind so that his face is hidden. The voices of THE DAMNED call out again, on top of each other, over and over, harsh, menacing.)
CRONE	Just give me some of mother's ruin!
LINK BOY	Light your way, sir?
RESURRECTION MAN	A little of what you fancy does you good!
HARLOT	Looking for a good time, are you, dearie?
RESURRECTION WOMAN	Where's the money! Give me the blasted money!
BEDLAMITE	Hold him down! Keep him still while I finish the job!
	(The voices of THE DAMNED continue repeating their words, as HYDE raises his hand and offers it to JEKYLL. JEKYLL makes to take HYDE's hand and enter the doorway. Then, as if summoning a supreme effort, he cries out.)
JEKYLL	No! *(He turns from the doorway to the audience and speaks aloud, over the voices of THE DAMNED.)* I will call upon

---

Resurrection man/woman *Grave robber – person who, for money, stole dead bodies from graves to be used to teach anatomy (the structure of the body) to medical students.*

Bedlamite *A mad person; the term bedlamite originally referred to a patient at Bedlam, the Hospital of St Mary of Bethlehem, which became the first hospital for the insane in 1547.*

I will call upon the Lord . . . *Taken from the book of Psalms in the Bible.*

the Lord, who is worthy to be praised; so I shall be
saved from my enemies!   40

*(The voices of THE DAMNED fall silent. JEKYLL
continues.)*

Destroy, O Lord, and divide their tongues, let death
seize them, let them go down alive into Hell, for
wickedness is in their dwellings and among them.
What is man that you are mindful of him? And the
son of man that you visit him? For you have made
him a little lower than the angels and you have
crowned him with glory and honour.

HYDE   *(Sneering and mocking.)* What is man?   50

*(His voice seems to strike at JEKYLL like a knife in the
back. JEKYLL turns swiftly back to the doorway, but, as he
does so, the door swings shut. JEKYLL remains onstage,
facing the doorway, with his back to the audience.)*

 DISCUSSION One of the themes of the play is that of temptation, and
the struggle within ourselves between the 'good' and 'bad' sides of our
natures. As a class, discuss how this theme is dramatised in the
opening scene.

ARTWORK Taking into account the author's description of the set in the
'Introduction' (pages v–vii), sketch how you think the opening scene might look in
the theatre, at the moment when the figure of Hyde first appears in the doorway.
Think about the effect you want this scene to have on the audience, and the
atmosphere you want to create.

SCENE 2

Utterson's chambers

UTTERSON enters and speaks to the audience.

UTTERSON	My name is Utterson. I'm a lawyer, and I've known Dr Henry Jekyll for many years, as both a client and a friend. And in all those years, I have never known him be other than generous, considerate, affable, and, above all, a man of common courtesy and sensibility. I would have said that I, better than anyone else, knew the man. Until, that is, the incident of his will. And that was the occasion when I first came across the name of this . . . this damnable fellow, Hyde. Jekyll came to see me one day . . .

(JEKYLL turns to UTTERSON for a flashback scene. JEKYLL approaches UTTERSON, holding out a document towards him.)

JEKYLL	Utterson – I wonder if you would do me a favour.

(UTTERSON turns to JEKYLL.)

UTTERSON	As a friend, or as your lawyer?
JEKYLL	As both. I'd be most grateful if you would . . . take this into your keeping.
UTTERSON	What is it?
JEKYLL	It's my will.
UTTERSON	*(Taken aback.)* Your will? But you already have a will.

 affable *Friendly, good-natured.*

You and I
together . . .

JEKYLL   *(Cuts in.)* This
is a new will.
I want it to
replace the
other.

UTTERSON   I see.
I presume
you'll have
no objection
to my casting
a professional
eye over it?
Just to make
sure it's all in
order.

JEKYLL   I suppose it's
necessary.

30

40

UTTERSON   If you want me to take charge of it, Henry, I must
know what's in it.

JEKYLL   Very well, then. Here. Read it, by all means.

                  *(UTTERSON opens the will, looks down at it, then looks up
                  and speaks to the audience.)*

UTTERSON   So I opened the will, and I read it. And this is what I
read. *(He reads aloud from the document.)* 'In case of the
decease of Dr Henry Jekyll, all his possessions are to
pass into the hands of his friend and benefactor,

---

decease *Death.*

benefactor *A person who gives support (usually money) to another person.*

5

Edward Hyde. Moreover, in the case of Dr Henry Jekyll's disappearance or unexplained absence for any period exceeding three calendar months, the said Edward Hyde shall come into possession of, without prejudice or obligation, all rights, properties and monies . . . '

(He stops and looks up sharply at JEKYLL.)

UTTERSON	Henry, I don't understand this.
JEKYLL	It's perfectly plain, I think.
UTTERSON	You know it's not in my nature to question anyone's actions, or indeed their motives for those actions . . .
JEKYLL	Which is one reason for my entrusting you with that document.
UTTERSON	But the terms of the will are . . . unusual, to say the least. To give a man the right literally to step into your shoes . . . *(Trails off.)*
JEKYLL	. . . Should I be . . . *(Hesitates.)* . . . unaccountably absent for three months.
UTTERSON	But why? Why should you . . . disappear? And who is this man?
JEKYLL	You see his name written there.
UTTERSON	Edward Hyde. Do I know him?
JEKYLL	No. You don't know him.
UTTERSON	I have to say that I don't approve of this. I don't approve of it at all.
JEKYLL	And is that spoken as my lawyer or my friend?

without prejudice *Without harming a person's legal rights.*

unaccountably *Without reason or explanation.*

UTTERSON	As both. Henry, won't you tell me . . . ?
JEKYLL	I can tell you nothing, Utterson. Nothing at all. And I don't ask you to approve or disapprove. I simply ask you to take charge of the will.
UTTERSON	I don't know that I wish to.

80

JEKYLL	*(Suddenly impassioned.)* Please, Utterson. I urge you to. It is of the utmost importance to me, and to my peace of mind. Edward Hyde must be provided for.
UTTERSON	In all the years I've known you, you've never mentioned the name of Hyde. What is this man to you?
JEKYLL	He is . . . think of him as being as a brother to me. A long-lost brother. And if you are my true friend, you will take charge of that document – and of him, should anything happen to me.

90

	(There is a pause.)
UTTERSON	I can see you are determined.
JEKYLL	I am.
UTTERSON	Well, it's against my better judgement, and it will not rest easy with me but, for friendship's sake, I agree.
JEKYLL	Thank you. It's a great relief to me. You don't know how much. And Utterson, you are to speak to no one else about this. Do you understand? It is a private matter, between ourselves.
UTTERSON	Of course.

100

JEKYLL	Nor shall we speak of it again. After today, there will – there can be – no more discussion about the will, or

about Edward Hyde. Henceforth, that subject is closed.

(*JEKYLL goes off, leaving UTTERSON alone, with the will.*)

Henceforth *From now on.*

DISCUSSION The first scene is one of several 'non-naturalistic' scenes in the play, while the second is realistic – in other words, we can imagine it taking place in the real world. In groups, discuss the differences in how these two scenes are written, and what it is that makes one non-naturalistic and the other realistic.

Scene 3

Utterson's chambers

Sergeant KINCH enters and addresses UTTERSON.

KINCH	Is that the document there, Mr Utterson?	1
UTTERSON	Yes.	
KINCH	May I see it?	
	(UTTERSON hesitates.)	
	(Continues.) If you wish me to take the case . . .	
UTTERSON	I've betrayed Jekyll's trust already in speaking to you about it, so I suppose . . . yes, here.	
	(UTTERSON gives the will to KINCH, who reads through it quickly, then hands it back to UTTERSON.)	
KINCH	How long ago did Dr Jekyll give this document into your keeping?	10
UTTERSON	A little over six months.	
KINCH	And am I correct in assuming that it was then that your suspicions was aroused?	
UTTERSON	Not suspicions – not then. But I was . . . uneasy . . . about the whole business.	
KINCH	You was uneasy. But now you have your suspicions. Is that right, sir?	
UTTERSON	Yes, Mr Kinch.	
KINCH	*Sergeant* Kinch, if you'd be so kind, Mr Utterson. I was a detective sergeant in the police force before I . . . before we parted company, and I became a detective in a private capacity. And the title is one I still find it	20

	amenable to employ. The kinds of people I generally has dealings with, it gives me a little more influence with them.
UTTERSON	Very well, Sergeant Kinch. Yes. My suspicions now are most definitely aroused.
KINCH	To the extent you'll pay me the sum we agreed to follow this fellow Hyde, and find out what I can about him.
UTTERSON	Yes.
KINCH	Then if I may inquire of you further, Mr Utterson, what is it that has turned your unease into a suspicion? You've come across the man, have you? You've had dealings with him?
UTTERSON	No. And from what I've heard of him, I hope I never have reason or cause to.
KINCH	What have you heard?
UTTERSON	A story that fills me with the greatest fear for my friend's safety.
	(Pause.)
KINCH	If you'd be so good, Mr Utterson . . .
UTTERSON	It was quite by chance I heard the story. From an acquaintance of mine, Mr Richard Enfield.
KINCH	Indeed? He is a man of some . . . reputation. I'm surprised that someone like yourself, a respectable lawyer, should move in the same circles as Mr Richard Enfield.

I still find it amenable to employ *He still found it useful to use his old title.*

UTTERSON	Mr – Sergeant – Kinch, because I know a man does not 50 mean I share his mode of life. And I make it a steadfast rule not to sit in judgement over the deeds and character of my fellow beings. If I have a vice, it is that of extreme tolerance.
KINCH	But you make an exception in the case of Mr Hyde.
UTTERSON	Yes. After what Mr Enfield told me, I do. There is something in what he said . . .
KINCH	Which is something we still have to come to. Please continue with your story.
UTTERSON	Of course. As I said, it was quite by chance that Mr 60 Enfield told me of an incident that had left a particularly unpleasant impression on his mind. It happened about a month ago. He told me about it a few days later and I could see that he was still very much shaken by the whole affair.

(UTTERSON and KINCH move to the edge of the stage to witness the next scene, a flashback.)

WRITING Begin to write a character profile of Dr Jekyll, based on how he behaves and what he says in Scenes 1 and 2. Take into account what Utterson says about him in Scene 3. You may wish to discuss this in pairs or small groups first. Add to this profile as the play progresses so that, by the end, you have built up a detailed description of Dr Jekyll's character.

DISCUSSION Kinch doesn't tell us why he and the police force 'parted company'. In small groups, discuss why you think he left the police. Then share your ideas with other groups.

SCENE 4

The street where Jekyll lives, at night

ENFIELD and MARY enter, arm in arm, merry and laughing.

MARY	Really, sir! To say such things to a girl like me!
ENFIELD	Really, I would *only* say such things to a girl like you!
MARY	That's very bad of you, sir.
ENFIELD	I can't help it, my dear. I am, I'm afraid, a very bad man.
MARY	Perhaps I shouldn't be seen with you, then, Mr Enfield.
ENFIELD	Perhaps you're right. You have your reputation to consider, after all. Therefore, we should retire to some place a little more secluded.
MARY	My rooms are close by.
ENFIELD	I know they are. And I think they are the very place. But first – a little drink.
	(He takes a small flask from his pocket and unscrews the top. He goes to drink from it.)
MARY	Ladies first, Mr Enfield.
	(ENFIELD looks at MARY consideringly, then drinks first from the flask. He then hands it to her and she drinks. During the above, HYDE enters on the opposite side of the stage, partly in shadow, wearing a hat and a coat with the collar turned up so that his face cannot be seen. He also carries a walking-stick. He observes ENFIELD and MARY. Now, HYDE starts to make a move towards them. But, as he does so, a LINK BOY enters and stops him.)
LINK BOY	Light your way, sir?

HYDE	What?
LINK BOY	Light your way home, sir? Or wherever you're going. The streets are dark, sir.
HYDE	I know they are.
LINK BOY	And dangerous too. I'll light them for you.
HYDE	Out of my way.

30

(He tries to push past the LINK BOY, but the LINK BOY steps in front of him.)

LINK BOY	It won't cost you much, sir.
HYDE	It'll cost you much if you persist.
LINK BOY	Please, sir. Let me light your way.
HYDE	Light my way, will you? I'll light your way, you devil! I'll light your way to Hell!

(He raises his walking-stick and knocks the LINK BOY down. The LINK BOY cries out. ENFIELD and MARY turn to see what's happening.)

40

13

ENFIELD	What's going on?
LINK BOY	Don't hit me, sir!
	(HYDE raises his walking-stick to strike him again.)
MARY	No!
ENFIELD	Stop!
	(HYDE turns to face ENFIELD and MARY. They approach him.)
	(Continues.) Leave that boy alone!
HYDE	You know him, do you?
ENFIELD	No.
HYDE	Then what business is it of yours?
MARY	I know him. Come here, Tommy.
LINK BOY	Mary!
	(She goes across to him and helps him up.)
MARY	Are you all right?
LINK BOY	Yes. He was going to kill me, Mary. I saw it in his face!
HYDE	You're right, boy. I would have done, and thought nothing of it. If this . . . gentleman and his ladyfriend hadn't come interfering where they'd no business to.
ENFIELD	Who the devil are you?
HYDE	Hyde's my name. Edward Hyde, at your service.
	(He takes off his hat and makes a mocking bow.)
MARY	*(Starts as she recognises him.)* You!
HYDE	Me, indeed. How is business these days? Not so good? Poor pickings, I see.
ENFIELD	You know this man?

5

6

HYDE	Oh, yes. She knows me, don't you?
MARY	Yes. And I wish to God I didn't. *(To the LINK BOY.)* Come on, Tommy. You come with me. We'll get that wound bathed. And the sooner we're away from him the better.

70

(MARY helps the LINK BOY off. ENFIELD calls after her.)

ENFIELD	Mary!
HYDE	*(Laughs.)* I seem to have spoiled your night's pleasure, Mr Enfield.

(ENFIELD turns to him.)

ENFIELD	How do you know my name?
HYDE	I know you, Mr Enfield. Who doesn't? Your reputation goes before you. And now you know me, and we're both acquainted. So, if you'll step aside . . .

80

ENFIELD	What about the boy?
HYDE	What about him?
ENFIELD	Some reparation is owed for the harm you've done him.
HYDE	Reparation? For a wretch like that?
ENFIELD	As a gentleman – I assume you are a gentleman . . .
HYDE	No, Mr Enfield! I am not a gentleman!
ENFIELD	I demand you make some amends!
HYDE	Let me pass.

(HYDE pushes past ENFIELD. ENFIELD grabs his arm.)   90

reparation *Compensation to make up for harm or damage done.*

ENFIELD   You shall not.

                      (*HYDE turns on him furiously.*)

HYDE   Take your hand from me!

                      (*HYDE savagely half-raises his walking-stick at ENFIELD.
                      Shocked and frightened, ENFIELD steps back. Then, HYDE
                      lowers his walking stick and takes some coins out of his
                      pocket.*)

HYDE   Here. Buy your conscience with this. It's more than it's
                      worth.

                      (*HYDE throws the coins on the ground, then goes to the
                      centre door. He takes out a key, opens the door and turns.*)

                      (*Continues.*) Goodnight, Mr Enfield.

                      (*HYDE goes in through the door and closes it firmly behind
                      him. ENFIELD stares at the door for a while, then bends
                      down, and picks up the coins. As he's doing this,
                      UTTERSON and KINCH come forward again.*)

UTTERSON   (*Addressing KINCH, as if continuing their conversation.*)
                      But it was not the violence of the incident alone that
                      shook Enfield, though that, in its way, was bad
                      enough. It was the character of the man, his very
                      presence that unnerved him more than anything.

ENFIELD   (*Addressing the audience.*) It was evil. In his face, a look
                      of pure evil. A face that was hardly human. The face of
                      a beast. And his eyes shining with the very essence of
                      evil.

                      (*ENFIELD goes off.*)

DISCUSSION In Scene 3, Kinch says of Enfield 'He is a man of some . . . reputation'. Discuss what you think Enfield's reputation is, and his character generally, based on what you see of him in Scene 4.

ARTWORK Imagine Scene 4 is a scene in a film. Sketch a still from the film showing what you think is one of the key moments in the scene. Around your sketch, make notes on what the characters are saying at that moment and whether you think it should be filmed long-shot (from a distance), medium-shot or close-up.

IMPROVISATION Work in groups of three. Each take on one of the following characters:
- **a** Enfield
- **b** Mary
- **c** The link boy.

In turn, tell the story of what happens in Scene 4 from your point of view. You could then go on to either:
- **a** hot-seating – the rest of the group can question each character in turn to find out more information
- **b** writing a monologue by one of the above characters, telling their own version of the scene.

SCENE 5

The street where Jekyll lives, at night

UTTERSON   *(Addressing KINCH.)* There is one thing more. I asked Enfield to take me to the place where the incident happened. It's an area of narrow streets and cramped courtyards, with doorways leading into the rear entrances of several large houses. *(As he speaks, he moves towards the centre doorway.)* He showed me the doorway through which Hyde had gone. *(Points to the door.)* I stood before it. I knew where it led. To the house of my friend, Henry Jekyll.

KINCH   You fear some dark design, Mr Utterson?

UTTERSON   *(Turning back to KINCH.)* I do. That a man like Henry Jekyll – a fine man, Sergeant Kinch, a good man – that he should have any connection with this . . . creature . . . The thought of what that connection might be fills me with fear and foreboding.

KINCH   We are talking of a man who appears to be of a violent and villainous disposition. We are talking of a man having more than a passing acquaintance with Mr Henry Jekyll. Of that man having, shall we say, an influence over the said Henry Jekyll. An influence that

You fear some dark design *Utterson is afraid that Hyde has some secret power over Jekyll.*

foreboding *A sense of something bad about to happen.*

villainous disposition *Wicked nature or personality.*

having more than a passing acquaintance *Knowing somebody quite well.*

	may, you suspect, be of a criminal nature. Do I have your drift, Mr Utterson?
UTTERSON	Yes.
KINCH	And you wish me to . . . investigate this Mr Hyde, and to discover what I can about the nature of his influence on your friend?
UTTERSON	That is correct. And I wish you also to be discreet, Mr Kinch . . .
KINCH	Sergeant Kinch.
UTTERSON	I'm sorry. Sergeant Kinch. Your discretion is of the utmost importance. It is that, as much as anything, I am paying you for.
KINCH	And paying for it handsomely, if I may say so, Mr Utterson.
UTTERSON	That's no matter. But it is vital that Dr Jekyll knows nothing of your investigations – and nor should anyone else. His good name and reputation must suffer in no way at all.
KINCH	Of course. And if, in the course of my investigations, I discover things about Hyde that confirm all your suspicions?
UTTERSON	Then I shall decide how to proceed with the business. Until then, simply gather what information you can.
KINCH	It shall be done. You have chosen the right man for the job. Chosen – perhaps – the *only* man for the job. I know this city. I was brought up to her. She has been a suckling mother to me and has unfolded to me all

30

40

---

 paying for it handsomely *Paying a high price.*

her deepest iniquities, her darkest secrets. Whatever there is to be uncovered, Mr Utterson, I shall uncover it. I shall track this man down. I shall flush him out. He will not – if you will forgive the pun, hide from me. For if he is Mr Hyde, I shall be Mr Seek – and find!

UTTERSON I'm glad to hear it. I put all my trust in you, Sergeant Kinch. And not only mine. I also put the trust of Henry Jekyll in your care. Value it. Value that trust above all. For it is the trust of a good man.

(KINCH and UTTERSON go off, separately.)

iniquities *Wicked things.*

pun *A joke; a play on words.*

WRITING Imagine you are Kinch, and that you keep a journal (diary). Write an account of the job you've been given to do, and all that you know about the case so far. Include in this journal a description of Utterson and your opinion of his character.

HOT-SEATING One of you take the role of Utterson; the rest question him on his feelings at the end of Scene 5. You could ask him about what he believes to be the relationship between Jekyll and Hyde at this point in the play.
● Who or what does he think Hyde is?
● Does he trust Kinch to find out the truth?

SCENE 6

A child's bedroom, at night

JANET enters, and speaks to the audience.

JANET	A good man. Of course he's a good man. He was brought up to be, and I know that more than anyone. For it was me that brought him up. Not his mother and his father, no. Too busy they were. Him with his business, and her with her fine friends and her society gatherings. The poor little mite would have grown up a lone, lorn and loveless child, if they hadn't engaged me to be his nurse. *(YOUNG JEKYLL enters.)*	1
YOUNG JEKYLL	Janet! Janet! Will you tell me a story?	
	(JANET turns to YOUNG JEKYLL.)	10
JANET	A story you want, is it?	
YOUNG JEKYLL	Yes! A bedtime story?	
JANET	Have you washed your hands and face?	
YOUNG JEKYLL	Yes!	
JANET	Have you said your prayers?	
YOUNG JEKYLL	Yes!	
JANET	I wonder if you have.	
YOUNG JEKYLL	I have!	
JANET	Then say them again, so that I know for sure. Kneel	

 lorn *Desolate, forlorn.*

	down. *(She and YOUNG JEKYLL both kneel.)* We'll say them together. *(Both close their eyes as JANET prays.)* 'In you, O Lord, I put my trust. Let me never be ashamed; deliver me in your righteousness. Bow down your ear to me, deliver me speedily; be my rock and my refuge, a fortress of defence to save me. For you are my rock and my refuge. For you are my strength. Into your hands I commit my spirit. You have redeemed me, O Lord, God of truth. Amen.'
YOUNG JEKYLL	Amen.
JANET	Now, say a prayer for your mother and father.
YOUNG JEKYLL	And you, Janet. I'll not forget to say a prayer for you.
	(JANET rises and speaks to the audience as YOUNG JEKYLL prays silently.)
JANET	Mother and father to him, I was, as well as his nurse and his teacher. His body and soul were placed in my care, and I nurtured them both, to the best of my abilities. For it's a fallen world we live in, and the great enemy lies in wait to ensnare us all. *(Quotes.)* 'He sits in the lurking places of the villages, in the secret places he murders the innocent.' *(Continues.)* A hard world it is, to be sure, for the young and innocent. And so I brought him up with two aims in mind. To feed his mind, and to fear his God.
	(YOUNG JEKYLL looks up and stands.)

In you, O Lord, I put my trust . . . *Taken from the book of Psalms in the Bible.*

righteousness *Morally correct, virtuous.*

nurtured *Lovingly cared for.*

a fallen world *A wicked world, full of sin.*

the great enemy *The Devil.*

YOUNG JEKYLL	I've finished. Now will you tell me a story?
JANET	What kind of story is it you want?
YOUNG JEKYLL	A crawler.
JANET	A crawler? Where did you learn such an expression?
YOUNG JEKYLL	From you, Janet!
JANET	I'm sure you didn't. And I'm sure I don't know what you mean by it.
YOUNG JEKYLL	Yes, you do. A tale of ghosts and goblins, devils and demons. Stories of evil spirits and the dead that walk by night.
JANET	Oh! One of those stories, you mean?
YOUNG JEKYLL	Yes!
JANET	All right, then. Come and sit down, and we'll have a crawler!
	(YOUNG JEKYLL and JANET sit together. As they continue speaking, JEKYLL enters and observes JANET and YOUNG JEKYLL, as if watching a vivid memory taking shape before him.)
	(Continues.) This is a story my grandmother told me, and she said it happened when she was a girl.
YOUNG JEKYLL	Is it true, then?
JANET	Of course it's true. My grandmother was a God-fearing woman and she never lied. Now, in the village where she lived there was a young woman. She was a pretty creature, but she had a flighty mind, with too much care for the pleasures and trinkets of this world, and a

50

60

70

A crawler *A ghost story, to make the flesh crawl. Robert Louis Stevenson used the term for some of the stories he wrote.*

head too easily turned by a flattering word. And, as you know, those that give themselves too much to this world are well on the way to giving themselves to the devil. And that's just what happened to her . . .

(JANET's voice drops and becomes inaudible to the audience as JEKYLL begins to speak to the audience.)

JEKYLL   I see us as we were then, those many years ago, sitting close together in my room, where the candle flickered and the shadows gathered, and outside the window the moon rode full and high in the darkening sky. And across the deep chasm of the years, I can hear her voice, with its gentle cadences and soft country tones, speaking to me of the horrors of the supernatural world.

(JANET's voice becomes audible again, continuing the story she is telling YOUNG JEKYLL.)

JANET   . . . And her laughter was like no woman's laughter. Indeed, it was like no human laughter at all. A deep, dooming laugh it was, as if rising up from the bowels of the earth, from the bottom of Hell itself. And her eyes had become the eyes of a beast. And the people knew then that some damned and terrible thing had taken possession of her . . .

(JANET drops her voice and becomes inaudible as JEKYLL again speaks to the audience.)

flighty *Frivolous, not very sensible.*

give themselves too much to this world *Spend too much time enjoying life's pleasures, rather than trying to live a 'good' life.*

across the deep chasm of the years *Over a period of many years.*

cadences *Rising and falling sounds and rhythms.*

JEKYLL

And it was those stories, of Hell's hauntings and demonic possession, of human weakness and desire and damnation, that gave me my first glimpse of a vast world beyond the narrow confines of the one that daily occupies our waking minds, a world where the human soul itself was the battleground between the forces of good and the forces of evil – and where, all too often, evil prevailed.

100

JANET

(Raising her voice.) . . . And the last that was ever seen of her was one night up on the hilltop, where she was dancing by the light of the moon. And she was not dancing alone. For there was a man with her – or something that had the appearance of a man – and the two of them were dancing there together, hand in hand, going round and round and round. And the two of them danced their way off that hilltop, and she was never seen in this world again. But it was everybody's opinion – and my grandmother's no less – that the young woman had danced herself all the way to Hell, and it's in the fires of Hell she's dancing still.

110

JEKYLL

(Addressing the audience.) Dancing in the fires of Hell. Dancing in the moonlight with the devil. That image haunted me then, and haunted me through all the days of my growing up. It haunts me still. A terrible, terrifying image. But attractive too. And this question, no less than the image, haunted and haunts me today. If evil is so terrible, why is it also so attractive? Why does it draw us to it? To dance in the moonlight with the devil. Why do so many make that choice?

120

---

demonic possession *Being taken over by evil spirits.*

beyond the narrow confines *The stories gave Young Jekyll a view of life outside his own experience.*

prevailed *Won.*

(YOUNG JEKYLL speaks to JANET.)

YOUNG JEKYLL   Are there really devils in the world, Janet?

JANET   Oh, yes. You can be sure there are.

YOUNG JEKYLL   And among us too? In towns and cities?

JANET   In the brightest streets of the brightest cities, the devil walks. Doesn't the Bible tell us so? *(Quotes.)* 'For I have seen violence and strife in the city, day and night they go round on its walls; iniquity and trouble are also in the midst of it, destruction is in its midst; deceit and guile do not depart from its streets.' *(Continues.)* There. That's what the Bible says, and you know that the Bible is the true and holy word of God.

YOUNG JEKYLL   I've never seen a devil.

JANET   And how do you know you haven't?

YOUNG JEKYLL   I should think I'd know someone with horns and a tail.

JANET   And did the young man in the story have horns and a tail? Didn't he look like an ordinary, handsome young man? And wasn't that how he tricked the poor woman into giving up her soul to him? Deceit and guile, Henry. Those are the tricks the devil employs to trap us.

YOUNG JEKYLL   And is there just one devil, Janet?

JANET   One devil, but he has many servants. And of these there are two kinds to be wary of. There's the midnight demon and the noonday demon. The midnight demon comes with all the marks of Hell on his face, and he is

---

     in the midst of it *In the middle of it.*

guile *Cunning or sly behaviour.*

to be feared for sure. But the noonday demon is to be feared above him, for he walks abroad in the light of day, and though his soul is the soul of a fiend, his face is that of an ordinary man.

YOUNG JEKYLL   Is that in the Bible?

JANET   No. But it should be. And that's enough for tonight. No more stories. It's time for bed.

(JANET kisses YOUNG JEKYLL goodnight, stands, and moves away from him. YOUNG JEKYLL looks out towards 160 *the audience as JEKYLL approaches him and speaks. As JEKYLL speaks, HYDE enters, behind JEKYLL.)*

JEKYLL   The midnight demon and the noonday demon. It was the former that terrified me most. His footsteps I heard softly climbing the stairs, his hand opening the door, his formless figure entering my room, and standing above me, darker than the darkness, to lean forward and suck the breath from my mouth . . .

YOUNG JEKYLL   *(Cries out in terror)* Janet!

(JANET turns to YOUNG JEKYLL. He runs to her, and she 170 *folds her arms about him, hugging him.)*

JANET   *(Addressing JEKYLL.)* And when you ran to me from your night fears, I held you close and hugged and kissed your bad dreams away. And I told you nothing could harm you, because God was watching over you. For it's only our love of God and his love for us that protects us from the terrors and temptations of the fallen world. And I'd do the same now, if I could. I'd shield you from those terrors now, reach out to you from beyond my grave and be your guardian angel.   180

I'd do the same now, if I could . . . *Janet is dead, and it is her spirit speaking, saying that she would protect Jekyll from Hyde if she could.*

But I cannot. For I fear the love of God is far from your soul. And there's something that stands between us, there's a shadow that bars my way, and will not let me pass.

(She turns from JEKYLL, and makes her way offstage with YOUNG JEKYLL.)

JEKYLL   *(Calls out after her.)* Janet! *(Then swings round as HYDE speaks.)*

HYDE   She's gone, and there's no use calling her. She hears, but she cannot come. For it was me you called to first, and now I am here, and will not leave you.

(HYDE turns and goes offstage. For a moment, JEKYLL stares after him, then follows him.)

DISCUSSION Scene 6 shows a flashback from Jekyll's childhood. Discuss what you think the purpose of this scene is. What more do we learn about Jekyll's character? How does the scene develop one of the play's themes about the nature of good and evil?

WRITING We only hear the beginning and end of the story Janet tells to the young Jekyll. Using those as your starting and finishing points, write your own version of the whole story, then give it an appropriate title.

HOT-SEATING In small groups, one of you take on the role of Janet. The others question her, and try and find out:
- How she felt about Henry Jekyll.
- What she felt about his parents.
- If she thought she brought him up well.
- Why she was so concerned to protect him from 'the evil one'.
- What she felt about the society she lived in.

SCENE 7

The street where Jekyll lives

Through the other doors, THE DAMNED of the city enter, to take up positions around the stage. They speak to the audience.

RESURRECTION MAN	Look out of the window. Look into the night.	1
RESURRECTION WOMAN	Look out from the place where it's warm, safe and bright.	
LINK BOY	Look into the dark. What do you see?	
CRONE	Scraps of the dark are breaking free.	
BEDLAMITE	Scarecrow shadows in the city streets . . .	
MARY	Rag-men and women with rags on their feet . . .	
RESURRECTION MAN	The hungry, the homeless, the mad, the condemned . . .	
RESURRECTION WOMAN	The city's poor, the city's damned.	10
LINK BOY	With our empty hearts and our empty eyes . . .	
CRONE	With our voices humming like the buzzing of flies . . .	
BEDLAMITE	And the lump of our sins humped onto our backs . . .	
MARY	Like a grinning ape whose teeth are black.	
RESURRECTION MAN	We crowd the spaces where you dream in bed . . .	
RESURRECTION WOMAN	And our hollow faces fill your soul with dread . . .	
LINK BOY	And when you wake and hope we're not there . . .	
CRONE	And we've vanished like smoke in the morning air . . .	
BEDLAMITE	Look into the mirror; you'll know we're still here . . .	

MARY   Behind your reflection, the face of your fear.

                        (All go off, except MARY.)

DISCUSSION As a class, discuss what you think Scenes 6 and 7 are saying about the nature of evil in human beings.

ARTWORK Design costumes for two of the Damned of the city (the Crone, the Bedlamite, the Harlot, the Resurrection Man, etc.). Consider whether they should be realistic or more symbolic of what the character represents.

SCENE 8

Mary's lodgings

KINCH enters and joins MARY.

KINCH	You know this Mr Hyde, then.	1
MARY	Do I? Who says I do?	
KINCH	I say. And I know that you know him.	
MARY	And who are you?	
KINCH	I've told you. Sergeant Kinch.	
MARY	You ain't the regular law.	
KINCH	That's the truth. The very irregular law is what I am. As you're likely to find out if you don't play it straight.	
MARY	When has the law ever played it straight with me?	
KINCH	I'll play it straight with you, Mary, you can be certain of that. And I'll put it to you again. You know this Mr Hyde.	10
MARY	What if I do know him? What's it to you?	
KINCH	It don't mean nothing at all to me. But it does mean something to the gentleman I'm working for. And that gentleman is a gentleman of no small standing nor importance.	
MARY	Gentleman, is he? I've had to do with gentlemen, I have.	

 a gentleman of no small standing nor importance *An important, powerful man.*

31

KINCH	I can well imagine it. But you ain't had to do with this particular gentleman.
MARY	He's one of the few, then.
KINCH	Indeed he is. And he intends to stay one of the few. Which is why he has engaged me to have to do with you instead.
MARY	His errand boy, are you?
KINCH	Ain't we both of that kind, Mary? Don't people of their standing buy us and sell us both? For that's the way of the world, Mary, and that's how it stands with the likes of you and me.
MARY	What would you know about the likes of me and my world?
KINCH	More than you think. Enough to know that beneath the pretty mask you put on for your . . . customers, there's a soul that suffers. For it's a soul that's still pure, and that hates the mire it's sunk in – a soul that still knows the true love and faith of God.
MARY	*(Affected by this speech.)* How did you know . . . ? How do you know that?
KINCH	I see the crucifix about your neck. And I see the light of Eden shining out from your eyes.
MARY	*He* talks like that. He speaks to me of God and Heaven – and all the time it's Satan staring out from his eyes.
KINCH	Your soul's burdened. Tell me what troubles it.

mire *Swamp.*

crucifix *A cross worn by people of the Roman Catholic religion.*

the light of Eden shining out from your eyes *Kinch means that he can tell Mary is basically a good person, who tries to follow her religion.*

MARY	It's a long time since I was at confession . . .
KINCH	All the more reason, then. Come, child. Tell me all.
MARY	You're not a priest.
KINCH	I'm the best you've got.
MARY	And what if he was to find out I'd talked?
KINCH	How would he know?	50
MARY	There's nothing he don't know. He knows everything about everybody. And if he was to find out . . . the things he'd do to me . . . there's no human imagining.
KINCH	What's it worth?
MARY	What?
KINCH	What's it worth to you?
MARY	Talking business now, are we?
KINCH	Yes.
MARY	What's it worth to you?
	(KINCH takes some money out of his pocket and lays it on the table.)	60
KINCH	That much.
	(MARY counts the money.)
MARY	Anything else?
KINCH	You want more?
MARY	I fetch a high price. My customers usually give me a little . . . token of their esteem. As a mark of my worth.

confession *Roman Catholics attend confession, when they tell the priest about any sins they have committed.*

token of their esteem *a symbol of their respect or liking for her.*

(KINCH takes a bottle out of his pocket.)

KINCH   You can have that. Gin. One bottle. Which you'll get once you've told me all you know.

MARY   About Hyde?

KINCH   Yes.

(MARY picks up the money from the table.)

MARY   This is a fair sum of money. But it's not the first time I've seen such an amount. Some of the gentlemen who pay for my company pay highly indeed. There are two gentlemen in particular – both men of high standing. And though one would not care who heard his name spoke on my lips, another would be more than a little unhappy.

KINCH   He shall never know from me you spoke it. Who are these two gentlemen?

MARY   Mr Richard Enfield, and Sir Danvers Carew.

KINCH   *(Looking surprised.)* Sir Danvers Carew the politician; the highly respected, highly influential politician?

MARY   There's no other that I know of.

KINCH   So, these two pay regularly and highly for your services? What of it? I'm not paying you for idle tattle.

MARY   Be patient. I begin with them, but I end with Hyde. For it was through these two gentlemen that I made the acquaintance of another highly respected gentleman – and it's through him that I came to know Hyde. And may all their souls rot because of it!

---

 idle tattle *Gossip.*

DISCUSSION Discuss any differences you notice between the way Kinch speaks to Mary in Scene 8, and the way he speaks to Utterson. What do you think this tells you about Kinch's character? What do you think is his opinion of Mary?

SCENE 9

Mary's lodgings

KINCH moves to the side of the stage. CAREW and ENFIELD enter. ENFIELD carries a bottle and a glass. CAREW carries two glasses. They approach MARY and CAREW gives a glass to MARY. ENFIELD fills their glasses and they drink. MARY moves to join KINCH to narrate her flashback scene.

MARY	*(To KINCH.)* A little over eight months ago, I was . . . entertaining . . . these two gentlemen in my lodgings. The hour was late, and their spirits were high.
ENFIELD	*(To CAREW.)* She is a peach, is she not, Carew?
CAREW	A peach indeed, Enfield. A most rare and succulent peach.
MARY	*(Walking back to join them.)* It's very kind of you gentlemen to name me something I've never had the pleasure of.
ENFIELD	What? You hear that? Our dear Mary has never tasted a peach! You must rectify the situation, Carew.
CAREW	I intend to. Next time I shall bring you a whole basket of peaches, Mary. And once you have tasted them, they'll become your fancy, I think.
MARY	Well, you know what they say, sir – a little of what you fancy does you good!
ENFIELD	I'll drink to that.

narrate To tell the story of something that has happened, particularly when the event is being acted out in a film or play.

rectify the situation Sort out the problem; Enfield means that Carew should give Mary a peach.

CAREW   We shall all drink to that.

(*All drink, and then ENFIELD refills his glass and Carew's as MARY walks back to KINCH.*)   20

MARY   As they drank, there was a footstep on the stair and a knock at the door. Sir Danvers answered, and another gentlemen, who I did not know, entered the room.

(*A knock is heard.*)

CAREW   (*Moving towards the door.*) Here he is, Enfield! Didn't I tell you he'd come?

ENFIELD   You did. And the wager is yours. I'll pay up later, if I may.

CAREW   (*Opening the door.*) Naturally.

(*JEKYLL enters and he and CAREW shake hands. CAREW moves back towards ENFIELD.*)   30

ENFIELD   (*Holding out a glass to JEKYLL.*) Henry. Come in.   40

     wager *Bet.*

	Don't hover there in the doorway like a blessed ghost! Join us!
CAREW	Have a drink.
	(JEKYLL joins them. ENFIELD hands him a glass which CAREW fills from the bottle.)
JEKYLL	*(Taking the glass but not drinking anything.)* Thank you.
ENFIELD	What are you waiting for, Henry? Drink up! That's the finest claret.
CAREW	I should know. I paid a fine price for it. Drink.
JEKYLL	*(Sipping the wine.)* Yes. It is. It is very good.
	(ENFIELD turns to MARY, who moves back to join them.)
ENFIELD	Mary. Allow me to introduce you to my – our – good friend, Henry Jekyll.
JEKYLL	*(Looking anxious.)* Richard, please . . . !
ENFIELD	What's wrong?
JEKYLL	My name . . .
ENFIELD	Your name? He's worried about his name, Carew. Should he be? Are you worried about your name?
CAREW	Not a jot. *(To JEKYLL.)* Mary is a girl who can be counted on for the utmost discretion. Can't you, my dear?
MARY	Of course.
ENFIELD	You see? There's absolutely nothing to worry about, Henry. This room – this house – is a sanctuary, a most holy sanctuary.

claret *A type of wine.*

sanctuary *A place of peace and safety.*

CAREW	The sacred shrine at which we worship our goddess – Aphrodite.
ENFIELD	Here, you're safe from the prying eyes of the world outside. All appearances can be shed like so much dead skin. Here, you can be what you truly are. What you truly wish to be.
JEKYLL	Is that possible?
CAREW	Oh, yes. It's possible. More than possible. I can vouch for that. And I'll drink to it as well.
	(CAREW drinks deeply.)
ENFIELD	Don't look so serious, Henry! This is a house of joy and pleasure. Indulge yourself for once. Live a little. As I've told you before, my friend, you need to.
CAREW	And tonight, you will.
	(CAREW and ENFIELD drain their glasses and put them down. ENFIELD gives the bottle to MARY.)
ENFIELD	Look after him, Mary.
	(ENFIELD and CAREW go off, leaving JEKYLL alone with MARY. She pauses for a moment, then approaches him.)
MARY	And what will be your pleasure, sir?
JEKYLL	My pleasure? *(He drains his glass.)* Another drink.
	(MARY fills his glass again.)
MARY	And . . . will that be all your pleasure?
JEKYLL	*(Quickly.)* Yes! Yes, that will be quite all!

70

80

90

Aphrodite *The Greek goddess of love and desire.*

vouch for *Answer for; Carew means that he can prove that it is possible.*

(*He turns away from MARY but remains onstage, his back to MARY and KINCH.*)

MARY   (*Walks over to join KINCH and says*) And though he stayed the rest of that night, there was hardly another word passed between us. For the most part he just stood, looking out of the window, and sighing sometimes, as if there was some great sadness in him. Then, when the sun rose, he turned to me, and smiled, and thanked me for my company, and left.

KINCH   And it was the same on all the subsequent occasions?

MARY   The same.

KINCH   How many occasions in all?

MARY   I can't remember. Quite a few over the following months. He'd always arrive very late at night – sometimes in the early hours of the morning, when it was quietest. I knew it was him. I could tell by the gentle tapping at the door. And sometimes he'd bring a bottle of wine with him – always the best – and sometimes a little gift for me.

KINCH   And he was content simply to pass the time in your company?

MARY   Yes. And for my part I was more than content that he should. For he was the only man I ever knew not to ask anything of me. Who seemed to . . . like me for my own self, and not what I could give. Or sell. He was a real gentleman. A gentleman – and a gentle man, if you know what I mean.

KINCH   Did you talk?

subsequent occasions *Occasions that followed after.*

40

MARY	We talked.	120

KINCH   What about?

MARY   Nothing much, really. He asked me about myself, and I told him. And sometimes he spoke to me a little of his own life, his childhood especially. But nothing of any great consequence. Except, once . . . *(Tails off.)*

KINCH   Yes?

MARY   *(Hesitantly.)* I told you how I thought there was a kind of sadness in him. A heaviness in his heart. One time – it was the last time I saw him – this . . . heaviness seemed to be weighing more on him than usual. He 130 was very agitated. He hardly spoke a word to me. Just stood there by the window, looking out into the night. And then suddenly he turned to me, and he spoke – he spoke with such passion and rage . . .

(JEKYLL turns suddenly and cuts in loudly.)

JEKYLL   We're all beasts! Every man! The Beast dwells deep within us all. And sometimes not so deep. Our hearts are its hunting-ground, our souls are raked and scoured by its claws. Have nothing to do with us! We feed on the weak and the innocent. Fear us, hide from us, for 140 we'll destroy you! Destroy and devour you, and then destroy and devour ourselves!

(MARY walks over to JEKYLL and they remain still, holding each others' gaze, as UTTERSON enters and speaks to KINCH.)

UTTERSON   An odd thing for him to say.

?   consequence *Importance.*

KINCH	*(Turning to UTTERSON.)* Was it?
UTTERSON	If you knew Jekyll . . . quite out of character.
KINCH	Unless he had by then come under Hyde's influence.
UTTERSON	You think so?
KINCH	From what the girl told me, yes.

(KINCH turns back to MARY. She speaks to him, though keeping her eyes on JEKYLL. UTTERSON observes the scene.)

MARY But it wasn't his words that frightened me so much. It was his look. The look in his eyes. Such a look I'd never seen before, and hoped never to again. But I did. I have. I've seen it many times since then, and not softened by the face that holds it.

(She continues to hold JEKYLL's gaze as KINCH speaks to her.)

KINCH Where have you seen that look again?

MARY In the eyes of the other. In Hyde.

(JEKYLL turns suddenly away from MARY and goes off.)

(Continues.) As I said, that was the last time Dr Jekyll came to see me. And it was shortly after that I first encountered *him*.

KINCH Hyde?

MARY Yes. And what devil it was bound their two lives together, I'll never know. The one a man of such gentleness, and the other – hardly a man at all.

KINCH What makes you so certain they knew each other?

MARY He told me. Hyde told me. That first time. After he'd . . . done with me.

(HYDE enters and MARY walks to meet him as UTTERSON and KINCH watch from the side of the stage.)

HYDE   *(To MARY.)* I must compliment my friend Jekyll on his tastes. And thank him for introducing me to you.

MARY   You know him?

HYDE   Oh, yes. I know him. We are both very well   180
acquainted. On the closest of terms, you might say.

MARY   Shall I see him again?

HYDE   No. I don't think you will. He's done with you. Had all he wants. Which wasn't much, from what I can gather.

MARY   I'm sorry for it. I liked him.

HYDE   Liked him, did you? Meaning you don't like me, eh? Don't bother to deny it. I can see you don't. It doesn't matter. Who you like or dislike is of no consequence to you and your kind. It's who pays that counts, isn't it?

MARY   Yes.   190

HYDE   And I have paid very handsomely for your services. Haven't I, eh?

MARY   Yes.

HYDE   Yes. So think no more about Jekyll. He's gone from your life. And I have come into it. And I mean to stay for some time. So you'd better get used to it. And, if nothing else, you must agree, my dear, that of the two of us, I am the more . . . invigorating. Eh? Yes. *(Turns to go.)* I'll see you again.

MARY   Will you tell him . . .?   200

invigorating *Giving strength and vitality; Hyde means that he has more life in him than Jekyll does.*

(HYDE wheels round on her in a fury and interrupts.)

HYDE

I'll tell him nothing! He wants to hear nothing from you! You're dead to him! Do you understand that? Dead! And don't speak of him to me again! Don't mention his name again! Or you'll find me not so gentle!

(MARY steps back from him in fear. He holds her gaze for a moment, then turns and goes. MARY turns to KINCH.)

MARY

And since that time . . . since I first met him . . . I haven't had a peaceful day . . . or night. Every moment I live in terror of him. Even now, I wonder if he's not near, somehow watching us, hidden in some secret place – waiting for you to go . . . and then I'll hear his tread on the stair, see the door open, and him standing there . . . see his face . . . and it will be the last thing I see.

21

KINCH

What are you saying?

MARY

It will be a relief – when it happens. For I'll be free of him, then. It's the only way I will be free. *(Pauses.)* That's all I have to tell you. There's nothing more.

22

KINCH

Thank you. *(He hesitates a moment before continuing.)* If there's anything I can do . . .

MARY

What can you do for me? What can anyone? I must have committed some terrible sin in my life – some terrible sin – for him to be my punishment for it. Now, just give me that gin, and go.

(KINCH raises the bottle.)

KINCH

Te absolvo.

Te absolvo A Latin term meaning 'I absolve you'; these words were spoken by a priest at confession to show that a person has been forgiven their sins.

(He gives her the bottle.)

MARY   I'm beyond salvation. There's no priest on earth could   230
save me now. *(She drinks deeply.)* I've known him and
been defiled by him, and I fear my soul is damned and
lost forever.

(She drinks again, and goes off.)

> **beyond salvation** *Beyond help or rescue.*
>
> **defiled** *Made dirty; Mary means that she has sinned by sleeping with Hyde.*

IMPROVISATION Improvise a version of Scene 9 but, instead of
Mary, have a different character acting as narrator (i.e. Enfield, Carew
or even Kinch, after Mary has described the events to him).

DRAMA In pairs, devise and perform a scene in which Enfield first persuades Jekyll
to visit Mary.

DISCUSSION In small groups, discuss the attitude of Enfield and Carew to Mary.
 ● What is she to them?
 ● What do you think this tells us about the Victorian male attitude to women
   generally?
 ● Do you think our attitudes to women have changed since those times?

Report back your ideas to the rest of the class, then have a class discussion.

SCENE 10

Utterson's chambers

UTTERSON   Can we believe all that she's told you?

KINCH   You think she'd lie?

UTTERSON   Women like that . . .

KINCH   Women like that lie only when there is something to be gained. And what has been her gain? None. If you had seen her, Mr Utterson, you would have known, as I did, that in speaking to me she put herself at considerable risk. She goes in very fear of her life.

UTTERSON   Very well. But despite that, we are no nearer to knowing anything of real import about Hyde.

KINCH   On the contrary. I have stood in the room where he has stood. I have spoken to one who has . . . come into contact with him. I have felt his presence. A presence most strong. And, while I can't say I have a clear picture of the man, I do have an impression. A distinct impression.

UTTERSON   Impressions are all well and good, Sergeant Kinch. But it's facts we want.

KINCH   And facts you shall have. My enquiries, after all, are only just begun.

UTTERSON   And where will your enquiries lead you next?

KINCH   I believe Dr Jekyll is acquainted with a Mr Lanyon.

 of real import *Of real importance.*

UTTERSON	The surgeon, yes. They were at medical school together.
KINCH	I intend to go and see him.
UTTERSON	What for? He and Jekyll were good friends once, but they haven't spoken for some time. I don't see what purpose can be served in talking to Lanyon.
KINCH	There may be none. Then again, there may. You must leave me to follow my nose, Mr Utterson, which has some experience in these matters.

30

UTTERSON	That's what I'm paying for, I suppose. Very well. Make your enquiries where you will.
KINCH	Thank you. If we wish to get to the truth of this mystery, we must leave no stone unturned. And we must not flinch from whatever we find under it.

(KINCH and UTTERSON go off.)

Mr Lanyon *Although Lanyon is a doctor, he is referred to as Mr Lanyon, rather than Dr Lanyon, because he is a surgeon.*

WRITING Write entries for Kinch's journal, showing what you think he means when he says that he has felt Hyde's presence, and has a 'distinct impression' of him? Write Kinch's summary of what he has learned about Hyde so far and write his reasons for planning to interview Mr Lanyon.

SCENE 11

The street where Jekyll lives

JEKYLL enters and speaks to the audience.

JEKYLL	Each time I went to see Mary, I was filled with a desire that consumed my whole being. And a determination that this desire should be . . . fulfilled. And each time I failed. And each failure was an agony to me. I was tormented by . . . such thoughts . . . such terrible longings . . . My soul turned and twisted like a creature caught on a hook . . . I felt the life within me screaming for release. What was it that held me back, where others went forward without guilt or conscience? Went forward smiling to sin and be damned for it. Why could I not even think of sin, without being pierced through to the very roots of my being?

(JANET enters.)

JANET	That's enough, Henry! No more of this!
JEKYLL	*(Turning quickly to her.)* Janet? What . . . are you doing here?
JANET	I'm here to look after you, like always. Poor boy. You've lost your way. And you're in danger of losing your soul.
JEKYLL	My soul's in torment.
JANET	You've heard the noonday demon, Henry. You've listened to his voice. Didn't I warn you about him?
JEKYLL	It's a sweet voice, Janet.
JANET	And its sweetness will lead you to damnation.

JEKYLL	Perhaps I wish to be damned.
JANET	What? What are you saying?
JEKYLL	I wish to be damned! But it's only fear that keeps me from it.
JANET	Fear is also one of God's tools.

30

JEKYLL	Then He is a tyrant of a God if He must rule us through fear! And it's time to be rid of Him, I say! Be rid of Him, and be rid of fear . . .
JANET	Henry!
JEKYLL	And be rid of you!

(JANET stares at him for a moment.)

JANET   *(Stiffly.)* Very well. If that's what you wish. You shan't see me again. But I shall weep for you, Henry. I shall weep through all eternity for your poor, lost soul.

(She turns and walks off. JEKYLL suddenly weakens and calls after her)

40

JEKYLL   Janet!

(HYDE enters.)

HYDE   Leave her. Let her go. She died a long time ago. Let her rest in peace at last.

(JEKYLL turns to HYDE.)

JEKYLL   Who are you?

HYDE   The one who can set you free.

JEKYLL   Free . . . ?

---

tyrant *A cruel and dominant leader.*

HYDE	Of your fear. Of your guilt.
JEKYLL	How?
HYDE	I shall take your sins upon my shoulders. Suffer for you. Live for you. For I am that which cries out to be set free from bondage; I am the child lost in the forest of everlasting night; the thrill in the blood, the beat in the heart, the face behind the face in the dark mirror; I am the dark god howling and chained to the mountain; I am that which dwells eternal in all men. Come, my child. Unlock the door. Enter into your kingdom. Set me free, and live forever.

(HYDE opens the central door, and offers his hand to JEKYLL. We hear the voices of THE DAMNED calling out again, as in Scene 1.)

CRONE	Just give me some of mother's ruin!
LINK BOY	Light your way, sir?
RESURRECTION MAN	A little of what you fancy does you good!
HARLOT	Looking for a good time, are you, dearie?
RESURRECTION WOMAN	Where's the money! Give me the blasted money!
BEDLAMITE	Hold him down! Keep him still while I finish the job!

(The voices of THE DAMNED grow more and more insistent as, after a moment's hesitation, JEKYLL steps past HYDE and through the door. HYDE follows him, and closes the door behind them. The voices of THE DAMNED immediately fall silent.)

I shall take your sins upon my shoulders . . . *In the Bible, Jesus took the sins of the world on his shoulders. Hyde is posing as a sort of evil version of Christ. This is blasphemy (the sin of making fun of religion).*

dwells eternal *Lives forever.*

DRAMA This is another non-naturalistic scene, which is intended to dramatise the struggle within Jekyll between the forces of good and evil. In threes, devise and improvise the following scene: Character A is tempting Character B to do something Character B believes is wrong. Character C is trying to persuade Character B not to do it. When you're devising this scene, make your characters and setting as detailed as possible.

MIME/DANCE Mime or dance a version of this scene, showing in movement Jekyll's struggle between good (Janet) and evil (Hyde).

DISCUSSION In groups, discuss why you think the writer chose to repeat at the end of this scene the lines said by the Damned of the city in Scene 1. What effect do you think the writer is trying to create?

SCENE 12

Mr Lanyon's laboratory

LANYON and KINCH enter. LANYON pushes on a medical dissecting trolley. On the trolley is his medical bag. During the scene, LANYON opens the bag, and takes out various surgical instruments, arranging them neatly on the trolley. LANYON is speaking to KINCH as they enter.

LANYON	He was always speaking nonsense like that, as far back as I can remember. Waxing lyrical about the human condition. I told him he should have been a poet rather than a doctor. Poets can afford to shove their heads in the clouds and nose around up there. Doctors can't.
KINCH	During the time you were at medical school together, did he ever mention anyone by the name of Hyde?
LANYON	Hyde? No. Not that I can recall. He never mentioned anyone. Didn't have many friends. Only myself and Utterson. Rather a loner. Still is, from what Utterson tells me. Why all these questions about him? Is he in some kind of trouble?
KINCH	He may be.
LANYON	And this fellow you mentioned – this Hyde – he's involved in some way, is he?
KINCH	In some way. It is the nature of that involvement that I have been engaged to ascertain.
LANYON	I'd like to help you. Henry Jekyll and I may not have

dissecting *Cutting up in order to examine and find out more.*

Waxing lyrical *Speaking in poetic language; Lanyon is making fun of Jekyll.*

	spoken for some years, but I had the greatest respect for him. However, as I said, I've never heard of this Hyde.
KINCH	Tell me something more about Dr Jekyll's . . . theories. Those that you took such a particular dislike to.
LANYON	I didn't say that . . .
KINCH	You didn't have to.
LANYON	I don't see how it can help.
KINCH	Neither do I, as yet. But, as they say, every little helps. Grains of sand, Mr Lanyon. Grains of sand.
LANYON	What?
KINCH	They make a mountain eventually.
LANYON	Oh. Well, I don't really have much time. I have to prepare for tomorrow's demonstration.
KINCH	As much time as you can spare. I ask no more. Please – tell me about Dr Jekyll's theories.
LANYON	Very well. (*He pauses, thinking back.*) They weren't theories as such. Not what I'd call theories. Musings, more like. Daydreams. I had no time for them. I was always a blood and bones man. Whereas Jekyll was what you might call a mind and soul man. Always questioning the reason for this, the meaning behind that. Now, there's a place in medicine for a certain amount of scientific enquiry – as long as it's rooted in the practical. But Jekyll's enquiries, to my mind, weren't medical or scientific, and as far as I could see they weren't of any practical use whatsoever.

Line numbers: 20, 30, 40

ascertain *Find out.*

(As he speaks the last sentences, LANYON wheels the trolley to the side of the stage and disappears, in the shadows, although his voice can still be heard.) As I told you, we were students together at the hospital – both of us poor, as all students are – and it was Jekyll's suggestion that we earn a little money by working between our studies at the asylum.

asylum *Hospital for the insane.*

DRAMA We don't see the start of this scene, which opens when Mr Lanyon is already speaking to Kinch. In twos, devise and perform how you think the scene may have started, beginning with Kinch introducing himself to Mr Lanyon, and ending at the point where the scene currently starts.

SCENE 13

Mr Lanyon's laboratory

A BEDLAMITE rushes onstage, wild-eyed, dressed in rags, crying out in terror. He is a character from the flashback scene which is about to begin. KINCH moves away and stands at the side of the stage, observing the scene, as the BEDLAMITE rushes around the stage shrieking in terror.

BEDLAMITE	He bites! He burns! Help! He follows me! Don't let him get me! Help me! *(The BEDLAMITE crouches, staring about him.)* Still. Quiet. Ssh. *(The BEDLAMITE looks up and cries out)* The fiend! I see him! He comes. The foul fiend!	1

(He stands, staring off. JEKYLL, as a young man, enters and speaks to him.)

JEKYLL   Keep still! Stay there! Everything's going to be all right.

(JEKYLL takes a step towards the BEDLAMITE.)

BEDLAMITE	*(Terrified.)* The fiend! The foul fiend!	10

(He turns to run. JEKYLL calls out.)

JEKYLL   Lanyon! Stop him!

(LANYON enters, as his younger self, and makes a grab for the BEDLAMITE.)

BEDLAMITE   *(Screams.)* Away! The foul fiend follows me!

(He escapes from LANYON's grasp, only to be faced with JEKYLL.)

The fiend! . . . *The things the Bedlamite says are adapted from the speech of Edgar/Poor Tom in Shakespeare's play* King Lear.

(Continues.) Fire and flame! Whirlpool and quagmire! He bites! He stings! He burns my feet and freezes my blood! Defy him! Defy the foul fiend!

(During the following speeches, the BEDLAMITE keeps trying to dodge LANYON and JEKYLL, as they repeatedly block his path.)

LANYON   What has happened?

JEKYLL   He escaped. Attacked one of the warders and made a run for it.

LANYON   God knows where the poor devil thinks he's going.

BEDLAMITE   Away! Away from the fiend! He pursues me. He dogs my trail. Sometimes a hound baying for blood, he lifts his head and howls. Sometimes the master of the hunt, he cries out 'Tarantara! Hillo, there, Lightfoot! On, sir! To the chase!' and sometimes he comes as the foul fiend!

(The BEDLAMITE makes a break for it. JEKYLL grabs him and holds him as he struggles.)

JEKYLL   And who is he? Eh? Who is this foul fiend?

(The BEDLAMITE stops struggling and looks at JEKYLL.)

BEDLAMITE   Would you know his name, sir?

JEKYLL   Yes, I would.

BEDLAMITE   Then I must speak softly, in case he hears. *(He draws JEKYLL closer to him and whispers.)* His name is Legion, and he is many.

---

quagmire *A bog or swamp.*

Tarantara! Hillo, there, Lightfoot! On, sir! To the chase! *This is what a huntsman might call out to his hound.*

(The BEDLAMITE bites JEKYLL's hand. JEKYLL cries out in pain and looses him.)

JEKYLL   Lanyon!

(LANYON makes after the BEDLAMITE, but the BEDLAMITE pushes him aside.)

BEDLAMITE   Chase me, boys! You won't catch me! I'm away with the wind!

(He turns to run offstage, but the WARDER enters in front 50
of him, carrying a cosh and a strait-jacket, and hits the BEDLAMITE with the cosh, knocking him down.)

WARDER   Got you! That's knocked the wind out of your sails, my son. *(To JEKYLL and LANYON.)* You two – give me a hand, here.

(JEKYLL and LANYON help the WARDER to put the strait-jacket on the BEDLAMITE, who struggles to be free.)

BEDLAMITE   No . . . don't . . . He'll come for me . . . the fiend . . .

WARDER   Hold him still!

BEDLAMITE   . . . He bites . . . He burns . . . Chews your flesh and   60
gnaws your bones. See him . . . there . . . and there . . .!

WARDER   Hold him still, I say, while I finish the job!

BEDLAMITE   . . . The foul fiend . . . The foul fiend . . . He'll drag your soul to Hell!

His name is Legion, and he is many *This is said about an evil spirit in a story taken from the Gospel of Mark in the Bible. 'Legion' means 'many'.*

Warder *A person who acts as guard and nurse to patients in an asylum.*

cosh *A heavy, blunt weapon used for hitting people.*

strait-jacket *A garment which restricts the movement of a person's arms and was used to restrain mental patients.*

(The WARDER hits the BEDLAMITE again.)

WARDER   That's enough from you!

(The BEDLAMITE becomes still as the WARDER finishes fastening the strait-jacket.)

(Continues.) There. That's done it! All safe and secure again now. *(He drags the BEDLAMITE to his feet and addresses LANYON and JEKYLL.)* See how quiet he is, now? Quiet and peaceful as a lamb, ain't you, once you got your coat on. That's how it is with him, you see. He's only happy when he's all trussed up. He don't like to be free. Freedom's a torment to him. A gentle soul when he's strapped in his suit. But out of it – he's a terror on the streets. A regular savage. Not that he's much different to the rest of us. This strait-jacket's what you might call his conscience. What we have nurtured into us, he has to have strapped on his back. With it, you have a God-fearing soul. Without it – a regular savage. *(To the BEDLAMITE.)* Come on, my son. Time to go and have a nice lie down. And mind you say your prayers before you sleep.

(He takes the BEDLAMITE off. JEKYLL stands staring after him. LANYON moves to the edge of the stage to speak to KINCH.)

LANYON   It may have been working there that first gave him his ideas. The place affected him. Too sensitive, you see. Not enough iron in his soul. Poor Henry Jekyll had far too much in the way of imagination. Especially for having daily contact with a place like that. *(Turns as JEKYLL speaks to him.)*

 Not enough iron in his soul *He did not have a strong/tough enough personality.*

JEKYLL	It is conscience, I believe, Lanyon, that is the root cause.
LANYON	*(Walking back to JEKYLL.)* The root cause of what?
JEKYLL	The problem. The human problem.
LANYON	And what is the human problem, in your opinion?
JEKYLL	That we are fallen beings.
LANYON	Ah! You're venturing into metaphysics and religion again. Not my territory, I'm afraid. Nor should it be yours, as a man of science.
JEKYLL	The human problem is not a scientific or a religious one. It is a human one.
LANYON	You see – you've lost me already.
JEKYLL	Listen.
LANYON	If I must.
JEKYLL	I was thinking about what happened the other day. In the asylum . . .
LANYON	That fellow escaping.
JEKYLL	Yes. And something the warder said about the strait-jacket being his conscience.
LANYON	Yes. Rather a clever analogy, I thought.
JEKYLL	It's more than just an analogy. That warder hit upon a profound truth. That's just what a conscience is. A strait-jacket that holds fast all those base desires we've inherited from our savage ancestors. Desires and

100

110

---

metaphysics *The philosophy (theoretical study) of existence.*

analogy *A comparison.*

a profound truth *A deep truth.*

---

appetites they had need of for the brutal world they inhabited. But such appetites are incompatible with our more civilised world, and so we have learned to suppress them, keep them at bay.

LANYON And a good thing too, if you ask me.

JEKYLL But the point is we still have them. Down there in the cellarage of our beings, all those primitive cravings still exist, like some beast caged in the darkness.

LANYON Speak for yourself, Henry. I'm not aware of any beast caged within me.

JEKYLL I'm sure you're not aware of it. You have a firm disposition, strong moral fibre – a high opinion of your own worth.

LANYON I trust that is meant as a compliment.

JEKYLL It is. You have that strength of character that does not allow these primitive desires to surface. If you like, the beast is buried deep in you. So deep, you don't even know it's there. But with others, it's different.

LANYON The poor wretch in the asylum? The foul fiend?

JEKYLL Him, and others like him. Either their characters are too weak, or the desires are too strong. They cannot be held in check by the usual means. And we've both seen the result of that. The beast breaks out of its cage. It rises from the depths. It pursues them, and finally devours them. They become the beast themselves.

---

incompatible *Do not go well with.*

suppress *Hold back, restrain.*

cellarage of our beings *Deep inside us.*

primitive cravings *Basic desires.*

a firm disposition, strong moral fibre *A steady, strong personality.*

What was it the warder called him? 'A terror on the streets.' And there's enough terror on these streets of ours for us to know it doesn't manifest itself only in the insane. Walk down any dark thoroughfare at night. See the shadowy figures crouched in their corners. Hear the cries of hatred and anguish. The beast is free and walks everywhere.

(LANYON turns to speak to KINCH.)   150

LANYON   You must understand, Jekyll didn't formulate these ideas during the course of a single conversation. It was over several months, during the time leading up to our final examinations. That's what irritated me as much as anything. There I was, trying to study, with him all the time going on about these increasingly wild ideas of his.

(JEKYLL begins speaking again, and LANYON turns back to him.)

JEKYLL   It's a kind of base metal, corrupting our natures,   160
preventing us from becoming what we are meant to be.

LANYON   And what are we meant to be?

JEKYLL   The lords of earth and creation.

LANYON   Really, Henry, this is too much!

JEKYLL   No, hear me out . . .

LANYON   I've heard enough.

---

manifest itself *Show or reveal itself.*

formulate *Form/express.*

base metal *A low-value metal which is often mixed with other, more valuable metals; Jekyll means that the evil side of the human personality is mixed with the good side, and spoils it.*

JEKYLL	*(Raising his voice sharply.)* No, you haven't! You *will* hear me out!
LANYON	*(Taken aback.)* Very well. Go on.
JEKYLL	This base metal of our beings – the beast within us – cannot be eliminated so long as it remains a part of us. But if science could find a means whereby the savage man could be separated from the civilised man, our self divided into its good and evil parts, then the good would have the opportunity at last to flourish, and grow, and we would become what God intended us to be.
LANYON	And our evil selves – the beasts – what would become of them?
JEKYLL	They would be mere brute existences. The detritus of life. Without our civilising influence to nourish them, they would dwindle, diminish, and eventually become extinct. Then, the earth would be a true paradise.
LANYON	And all this can be brought about by science, you say?
JEKYLL	I'm convinced of it.
LANYON	And I'm convinced that this theory of yours has very little to do with science, and far more to do with fairy-tales.
JEKYLL	No!
LANYON	It's nothing but fancy. Pure fancy. Though, I must admit, it is a very well-thought through fancy.
JEKYLL	You can't just dismiss it like that.
LANYON	I can. And I do. And so should you. You'd do better to

detritus *Waste, unwanted remains.*

	devote your time to your proper studies.
JEKYLL	These *are* my proper studies, and I'll devote my life to them!
LANYON	I wish you well, then. But I fear your life will be a wasted one.
JEKYLL	*(Shouting angrily.)* I never realised you were so narrow and small-minded! But you'll see! I'll prove you wrong!
LANYON	*(Still composed.)* And I never knew, my dear Jekyll, that you had so much rage inside you. You really must keep it in check, you know.
	(For a moment, JEKYLL glares in anger at LANYON, then turns quickly, and goes off.)

200

DISCUSSION The character of the Bedlamite does not appear in the original book. As a class, discuss why you think the writer decided to create this scene. How do you think the character of the Bedlamite and the setting of the asylum add to the play?

DISCUSSION AND WRITING In this scene, Jekyll attempts to explain his theories to Mr Lanyon. These ideas are central to the whole play. Discuss what you think he means by these theories, and whether you agree with them or not. Then, look through what he says again, and try to write a summary of what he believes.

ARTWORK Choose what you think is the most dramatic moment in this scene and draw it as if it is a still from a film. On your drawing, write what the characters are saying at that particular moment, and state whether the moment should be filmed in long-shot, medium-shot or close-up.

SCENE 14

Mr Lanyon's laboratory

LANYON turns to KINCH, who joins him centre stage.

LANYON	Our friendship cooled somewhat after that. After we finished our studies we went our separate ways – he to a lucrative private practice, while I took a post here, at the hospital. Which you can see I still keep.
KINCH	And did Dr Jekyll pursue his . . . theories?
LANYON	I've absolutely no idea. Nor do I care. Theories are all well and good, but they don't benefit the world much. Quite the opposite. In my experience, most of the world's difficulties arise from some theory or other about the way it should be run.
KINCH	You might well be right.
LANYON	I believe I am. I'm a practical man, Sergeant Kinch, and it's practicalities that count. Getting your hands dirty. Do you know what I mean?
KINCH	Oh, yes, I know what you mean. I'm not averse to getting my hands dirty myself.
	(MARTHA and LAZARUS enter.)
MARTHA	Mr Lanyon . . .

---

lucrative *Profitable.*

averse *Opposed, not inclined.*

Martha and **Lazarus** *In a Bible story, Jesus raises from the dead a man called Lazarus who has a sister called Martha. In this play, Martha and Lazarus are grave robbers, 'raising the dead' out of their graves.*

(LANYON turns to them.)

LANYON	Yes?

20

MARTHA	*(Hesitantly, looking with suspicion at KINCH.)* We have the . . . er . . . item you requested.

LANYON	It's about time. You're late.

LAZARUS	We had a bit of trouble . . .

LANYON	Never mind about that. Bring it in. I have to prepare it for tomorrow morning.

(MARTHA and LAZARUS hesitate, looking nervously at KINCH.)

(Continues.) Well? What's the matter?

MARTHA	It's . . . all right, is it, Mr Lanyon . . . to bring in the . . . item?

30

LANYON	Of course it's all right! Oh, I see what you mean. You need have no concerns about this gentleman, I assure you.

LAZARUS	If you say so, Mr Lanyon . . . only, we all have to be careful, you know.

MARTHA	We'll fetch it right away.

(MARTHA and LAZARUS go. LANYON turns to KINCH.)

LANYON	Sergeant Kinch. I believe I've done you a favour in giving up my time to you – and speaking so freely.

40

KINCH	You have indeed, Mr Lanyon.

LANYON	So, I'd take it as a great favour to myself if you were to say nothing to anyone of the business at hand. This is a teaching hospital, as you know, and practical demonstrations are a daily requirement. They're fundamental to our work here. If the workings of the human body are to be fully understood, it's necessary

to examine and explore those workings at first hand.

KINCH   Do I take it that these demonstrations are of an anatomical nature?

LANYON   Exactly so. There's great demand for the raw material for these demonstrations, which can't be supplied by the hospital mortuary alone. Other sources must be found. It's a practical necessity.

(As he speaks, LANYON fetches the dissecting trolley and wheels it onstage.)

KINCH   Of course. I understand. Your favour shall be returned.

(MARTHA and LAZARUS enter, carrying between them a body in a sack.)

MARTHA   Careful! Don't drop it!

LAZARUS   I won't drop it!

MARTHA   You did on the way here. Twice! And Mr Lanyon don't want damaged goods, do you, Mr Lanyon?

LAZARUS   He won't get goods more damaged than this. Damaged beyond repair, they are!

(They struggle with the body and lay it on the dissecting trolley.)

MARTHA   But fresh, sir, fresh as a daisy. Left this earth last night. Put into it this morning. Took up out of it again tonight. You won't find much fresher than that.

LAZARUS   Not that it'll stay fresh for long. They don't, do they? Have a terrible habit of going off sharpish, these goods do. And sharpish is the word, if you take my meaning.

---

anatomical *Relating to anatomy – the structure of the body.*

mortuary *A place where dead bodies are kept before burial.*

LANYON	Well – let's take a look at it. *(He tries to untie the sack, but cannot.)* You've made this knot rather fast.
MARTHA	*(To LAZARUS.)* I told you. *(To LANYON.)* I'm sorry, Mr Lanyon. But my brother was, in his youth, a seafaring man, and he likes to show off his knots from time to time. Allow me.
	(She takes out a knife and cuts the cord. LANYON examines the body. During this, LAZARUS speaks to KINCH.) 80
LAZARUS	Would you be a medical man, sir?
KINCH	No. I wouldn't.
LAZARUS	Only, you have the look about you.
KINCH	And what look's that?
LAZARUS	An unflinching eye. An eye that can gaze without tear or tremor upon the body of mortality. And a nose that can smell it out.
KINCH	There's more than just medical men have a need for an eye and a nose like that. 90
LAZARUS	Indeed there is. Such as those of our profession. And yours, no doubt – whatever that may be.
KINCH	You're right – whatever it may be.
	(LANYON is now looking at the body, which we can't see.)
LANYON	Young. That's good. No exterior marks. *(To MARTHA.)* What was the cause of death?
MARTHA	Unknown, Mr Lanyon. Name unknown. Life unknown. Cause of death – unknown.

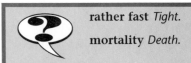

rather fast *Tight.*

mortality *Death.*

LANYON	Well, at least the poor creature will make a greater imprint on the world after death than was made before it. And bring some benefit too. *(He takes some money out of his pocket.)* It's a fine specimen. You've done a good job. Here's your payment.
	(He gives some money to MARTHA. During the rest of the scene, MARTHA and LAZARUS stand to one side, quietly counting their money.)
MARTHA	Thank you very much, Mr Lanyon.
LAZARUS	Thank you very much indeed, sir. A pleasure doing business with you – as always.
LANYON	Yes. And now, I'd better get on with the business in hand.
KINCH	Mr Lanyon. Might I be permitted to . . . view the item? Out of natural and professional curiosity.
LANYON	By all means, if you wish.
	(KINCH goes to the body and looks at it.)
	(Continues.) In a few hours' time what you see there will be nothing more than carved meat on a slab. So much poundage of flesh, blood and bone. All for a good cause, of course. The advancement of medical science.
KINCH	Of course.
LANYON	But this is what we all come down to. And no more than this. That's the reason I have no time for theories like Henry Jekyll's. I can show you the organs that made that body work in life, I can show you the muscles that moved its limbs, the arteries that carried its blood, I can show you the brain that ran the whole operation. But I can't show you the soul. I can't cut that out. Because it doesn't exist. Because this, this bag of bones, is all we are.

(KINCH moves away from the body.)

KINCH 'What a piece of work is man,' eh, Mr Lanyon?

LANYON Eh?

KINCH A quotation – from the Immortal Bard.

LANYON Oh. I'm sorry. I don't have much time for that sort of thing. *(He takes hold of the trolley.)* You must excuse me, now. I have to take this through to the theatre and prepare it for the morning's lecture.

KINCH Of course. Thank you for your time, Mr Lanyon. And the . . . information.   140

LANYON I don't know how much use it's been to you. Some, I hope. And if I do hear anything about this man . . . what's his name again?

KINCH Hyde. Edward Hyde.

(At the mention of Hyde's name, MARTHA and LAZARUS look up sharply.)

LANYON If I hear anything about him, I'll let you know.

KINCH It would be appreciated.

LANYON Well, goodnight, then.   150

KINCH Goodnight, Mr Lanyon.

(LANYON goes off, pushing the trolley.)

  the Immortal Bard *Shakespeare; the quotation is from his play* Hamlet.

DISCUSSION Martha and Lazarus are intended to be comic characters, almost a comedy double-act. As a class, discuss why you think the writer decided to introduce an element of comedy at this point.

MIME/IMPROVISATION Mime or improvise the scene as Martha and Lazarus manhandle the body back from the graveyard to Mr Lanyon's laboratory. Remember that they would need to avoid being seen by anybody and that Lazarus dropped the body twice on the way. Try to make the scene as comic as possible.

WRITING Mr Lanyon describes himself as a 'flesh and bone' man. What do you think he means by this? Look through Scenes 12–14 to find other words and phrases Mr Lanyon uses to describe himself. List all these, and then use them to write a character profile of Mr Lanyon. In your profile, make a comparison between him and Dr Jekyll, pointing out how they are different.

SCENE 15

Mr Lanyon's laboratory

As soon as LANYON has gone, MARTHA and LAZARUS approach KINCH, tentatively.

MARTHA	Excuse me. Mr . . . er . . .	1
KINCH	Yes?	
MARTHA	We couldn't help overhearing you and Mr Lanyon talking . . .	
LAZARUS	Not that we're in the habit of eavesdropping, you understand . . .	
MARTHA	. . . Only, we couldn't help overhearing you just then . . .	
LAZARUS	. . . And there was a certain name that was mentioned – a name it was seeming you wanted information about.	10
KINCH	You mean the name Hyde?	
MARTHA	Just so, sir. The name Hyde.	
KINCH	You know him?	
LAZARUS	We can't rightly say as we know him. Can't rightly say as we'd like to know him.	
KINCH	But you've heard of him?	
MARTHA	More than that. We've met him. Spoken with him. Had dealings with him.	
KINCH	When?	20
MARTHA	This very night, as it happens.	
KINCH	Tell me.	

LAZARUS	Now there you've hit upon a difficulty, sir. For while it is our utmost desire and intention to tell you, the matter is a delicate one . . .
MARTHA	What my brother means is, our dealings with this Mr Hyde was in the nature of a professional capacity, and them as works in our profession can't afford to be too free in speaking of it.
LAZARUS	It ain't that we're ashamed of it. It's a job that must be done. You ask Mr Lanyon there. Where would he be without us? Where would all them doctors in training be without us? Where would the whole blessed medical profession be without the likes of us?
MARTHA	And yet we must go in shame and in shadow. We must go in fear of the law. We, who raise the dead and bring hope of new life, treated as lepers and pariahs. It's an unfair and a hypocritical world we walk in, sir. Unfair, and uncommon hypocritical.
KINCH	I won't disagree with you there.
LAZARUS	Then you'll understand, sir, our hesitation in speaking so open and honest-like about our profession.
MARTHA	Especially to someone – meaning yourself – whose acquaintance we ain't had the pleasure of making. For in our position we can't be too careful who we go a-talking to.
KINCH	You need have no fear of me. I, too, am someone who must walk in the shadows. Sometimes some very dark shadows indeed. But perhaps this will help to bring a little light.

in the nature of a professional capacity *Through their work.*

lepers and pariahs *Lepers – people suffering from the disease of leprosy – and pariahs – Indian people of low caste (social standing) – have come to represent anyone who is a social outcast.*

(He takes out some money and gives it to MARTHA.)

MARTHA   It'll do. Tell him the story, Lazarus.

(During the following, HYDE enters, and stands to one side, turned away from them. As LAZARUS continues his story, MARTHA and HYDE enact the scene he relates. LAZARUS also partly enacts the scene with MARTHA and HYDE, while continuing to speak to KINCH.)

LAZARUS   Like my sister said, it was this very night we come across him. Me and Martha was out on this business for Mr Lanyon. And bleak-looking business it was. For though you might think there's an abundance of supply for the kind of merchandise we deal in, and though in the general sense you'd be right, in the particular sense that ain't always the case. 60

MARTHA   What Lazarus means is, we're after merchandise freshly manufactured, so to speak, and that's sometimes in short supply.

LAZARUS   As it was tonight. Not a fresh corpse could we find nowhere, though we'd searched near every blessed burying ground in the whole city. So, we come at last to a mean and miserable-looking place, all overgrown with briars and brambles. And it looked like most of its inhabitants had been there so long, they must've thought me and Martha was there to rouse them all for the last judgement. And I was just thinking to myself that we might as well give the whole thing up as a bad job, when all of a sudden, Martha turns to me and she says . . . 70

MARTHA   Look! *(Points to HYDE.)*

the last judgement *In medieval Christian belief, at the end of the world, the dead would be judged by God and either sent to Heaven or to Hell.*

LAZARUS	And I look, and I see a figure, a little way off, standing over one of the graves.

MARTHA	(To LAZARUS.) Who do you think he is?
LAZARUS	(To KINCH.) I didn't know, and I didn't care to know. The way he was just standing there, looking down at that grave,

when I swear there hadn't been nobody there before. As if he was a body rose up out of the ground itself.

MARTHA	(To LAZARUS.) Whoever he is, we don't want him seeing us. Come on, I think we'd best be out of here.
LAZARUS	(To KINCH.) But before we could make a move, he looks up, sudden-like, just like he's known we've been there all the time. And he says to us . . .
HYDE	Here!
LAZARUS	(To KINCH.) That one word. And we freezes, and he speaks again.
HYDE	Over here. This is what you're looking for.
LAZARUS	(To MARTHA.) Is he speaking to us?
MARTHA	I don't know who else. We're the only ones in this place can hear him.

LAZARUS	What shall we do?
MARTHA	There's only one thing, I reckon. Go and see what it is he wants.
LAZARUS	*(To KINCH.)* And before I can stop her, she's making her way towards him, and there's nothing else I can do but follow on behind.
	(MARTHA approaches HYDE, with LAZARUS hanging back.)
MARTHA	What do you mean? What might we be looking for? 120
HYDE	What else in this garden of rest? I know your trade.
MARTHA	Do you, now? And what trade might that be?
HYDE	*(Quoting.)* 'I am the resurrection and the life. He who believes in me, even though he dies, he shall live.'
LAZARUS	*(To KINCH.)* And the way he spoke them words, it made me go cold to the marrow of me bones. For there was more in the way of death about him than there was life.
HYDE	*(To MARTHA.)* I am correct, am I not? That's the commerce you deal in? Don't deny it. And don't ask me how I know. It's enough that I know, and that destiny has brought me here this night as your saviour. 130
MARTHA	Our saviour? And what might be the meaning of that?
HYDE	'Seek, and ye shall find.' Here, beneath this freshly turned earth, lies the treasure you seek.

I am the resurrection and the life . . . he shall live. *Taken from John's Gosepl in the Bible, in which Jesus talks to Martha about the death of her brother, Lazarus. Hyde is again posing as an evil Christ figure, and making fun of Martha and Lazarus.*

commerce *Business.*

destiny *Fate – a power that controls what happens to people.*

MARTHA	Someone you knew was it, sir? An acquaintance? Not, I trust, one of you own dear departed . . .?
HYDE	What concern is it of yours who the wretch was?
MARTHA	None, sir.
HYDE	Your only concern is to do what you came here for and dig it up.
LAZARUS	For the cause of medical science.
HYDE	For the cause of filling your pockets! Don't lie to me! I'll have none of your shuffling hypocrisy! Just get on with your work. And you'd better hurry. Mr Lanyon will be waiting.
MARTHA	You know him, do you?
HYDE	Who doesn't know the renowned Mr Lanyon?
MARTHA	If you're a friend of his . . .
HYDE	Who said I was a friend? He doesn't know me. Mr Lanyon will never have heard of anyone by the name of Hyde.
MARTHA	That's your name is it, sir?
HYDE	Yes. Edward Hyde. And now, Edward Hyde will leave you to your business. Goodnight to you both. *(He moves away, then stops, and turns back to them.)* Until we meet again.
MARTHA	And where will that be . . . Mr Hyde?
HYDE	Where all sinners meet. At the gates of Hell.
	(HYDE goes off. LAZARUS and MARTHA turn back to KINCH.)

saviour *A person who saves others; again, Hyde is posing as an evil Christ figure, because Christ is called the Saviour.*

LAZARUS   And he was gone, into the dark, like a creature born
                     out of it. And it ain't no lie if I say I could've sworn he
                     left the smell of brimstone behind him.

MARTHA   No, he wasn't no devil, brother. He was a man. Flesh
                     and blood. And to my mind there's the worst of it. For
                     never in all my life have I seen the face of mortal man
                     so etched with the marks of wickedness. Pure
                     wickedness, in every feature. And etched deep.

                     (They turn from KINCH and go off.)

brimstone *A symbol of Hell.*

etched *Marked by scratching fine lines.*

LANGUAGE Look closely at the way Martha and Lazarus speak in
Scenes 14 and 15. Compare the way they speak with the way Lanyon,
Utterson and Jekyll speak. Note down some of their phrases that show
this difference. In small groups, discuss what this tells you about their
characters.

DISCUSSION Martha says, referring to their work as grave-robbers, 'them as
works in that profession can't afford to be too free in speaking of it.' As a class,
discuss what she means by it. Go on to discuss what you think of grave-robbers –
do you think they were entirely bad or were they providing an important service?

HOT-SEATING One of you takes the role of Martha, while the others question her
about her profession. How does she defend the way she earns a living? Repeat this
exercise with Mr Lanyon – how does he defend his practice of buying bodies from
grave-robbers?

DRAMA Part of Scene 15 involves the action switching between Lazarus telling his
story to Kinch, and a flashback enactment of it. How would you present this scene
onstage, to make it clear to the audience what is going on? In groups of four, try
acting out that section in a number of ways, to try and find what you think would
be the best way of staging it. Begin at the point where Martha says: 'Tell him the
story, Lazarus.' and go on to the end of the scene. A number of groups could then
present their work to each other.

SCENE 16

Utterson's chambers

KINCH   *(To the audience.)* Pure wickedness, etched in every feature. If I'd sensed his presence before, I felt it strongly, now. Walking back through the night streets, I felt that presence like a shadow, creeping out from every corner and every doorway, and spreading across the whole of the city. And, at the centre of that shadow, a form, solidifying. His form – the figure of Hyde.

(UTTERSON enters.)

UTTERSON   *(To KINCH.)* You saw him?

KINCH   Only in a manner of speaking, Mr Utterson. I saw him here, in my mind's eye. *(Taps his forehead.)*

UTTERSON   Oh. I see.

KINCH   No, Mr Utterson. With respect, I think you do not see. I have become familiar with our shadowy friend. He is close – close to me. Almost within my grasp, so to speak. And the closer he comes, the more I feel that he is both less and more than an ordinary man. Quite extraordinary – if evil can be said to be that. All he touches becomes tainted by him. Corrupted! And whoever or whatever he is, his power is one to be reckoned with.

UTTERSON   And this is the kind of creature with which my friend Jekyll has become associated! It's hardly to be believed.

---

 tainted *Affected, tinged with something bad.*

Corrupted *Made bad.*

KINCH	I'm not so sure . . .
UTTERSON	What do you mean?
KINCH	According to what Mr Lanyon told me, even while he was still at medical school, Dr Jekyll had become interested in the nature of evil.
UTTERSON	You surely don't set any store by all that.

30

KINCH	Whether you or I or Mr Lanyon set any store by it is of no consequence. The point is that Dr Jekyll did, and stated his determination to devote himself to its study. Now, it may be that this Mr Hyde is somehow helping him in that study – and, in return, Dr Jekyll has taken him under his protection.
UTTERSON	If that's the case, I fear even more for him than I did before.
KINCH	So do I. For, whatever the nature of the pact between them, I fear it is a sinister one. Most sinister.

40

UTTERSON	Then what's to be done?
KINCH	What is already being done, Mr Utterson. We have entered the labyrinth. And we must continue to follow its winding paths until they lead us to the centre. And there we shall come face to face with the beast. And there, at last, I pray, we shall discover the truth about Hyde and Jekyll, and the secret bond that ties them.

(KINCH and UTTERSON go off.)

---

set any store *Consider important.*

pact *Agreement or deal.*

labyrinth *A complicated network of passages; Kinch means that the mystery of Jekyll and Hyde is a complicated puzzle.*

SCENE 17

Jekyll's laboratory

JEKYLL enters, carrying a glass flask, filled with liquid. He speaks to the audience.

JEKYLL
It was about a year ago that, after many failed experiments, I finally succeeded in isolating certain substances which, when mixed, had the power of bringing about chemical changes to the nervous system. And the effect of these changes was to strip away the outer shell of consciousness and release, from within, the inner spirit, and allow it to take full possession of the physical form. In other words, I had at last found a way of releasing the beast from its cage, and letting it walk free in the world. *(He pauses.)*

My ideas had changed much since my student days. Then, I had wanted to free the outer man from the tyranny of the beast. Now, I had come to see what a hypocritical, whining, ineffectual creature civilised man was. If we were to truly live – if I was to truly live – it could only be through the agency of the inner, hidden man. And it was this I looked forward to with trembling expectancy that first night, when I proposed to release that hidden man for the first time. *(He holds up the glass container.)*

The solution of chemicals was prepared. My elixir of life. I locked the door to my laboratory, fastened all the windows, lifted the glass to my lips, and drank.

---

through the agency of *Through the action or influence of.*

elixir of life *A magical substance said to cure all ills or to make somebody live forever.*

80

(He drinks the liquid. As he does so, HYDE enters through the central door. JEKYLL has his back to HYDE. HYDE speaks to the audience.)

HYDE Pangs of agony racked my body. There was a cracking of bones, a grinding of flesh, the pounding of blood through every artery and vein. I felt as if I was falling into an immense darkness, a darkness beyond death. 30 And, in the darkness, the beast howled, a long, terrifying howl of rage and release. And into that howl I fell, and was consumed, and there was silence.

(JEKYLL lowers the glass. He speaks to the audience.)

JEKYLL And as quickly as they'd arisen, these agonies subsided. I came to myself once more as if out of a great sickness, and when I looked about me, it was as if I were seeing for the first time. Seeing, hearing, feeling, all for the first time. Colours brighter. Sounds sharper. Senses keener. I was filled with an immense strength. 40 And joy! Such joy! I felt as if, for the first time in my life, I could do anything!

(HYDE speaks to JEKYLL.)

HYDE You shall. You shall do anything.

(JEKYLL turns to face HYDE.)

JEKYLL I turned to the mirror.

HYDE Anything and everything.

JEKYLL I gazed upon my face.

HYDE Without restriction or restraint.

JEKYLL My own features transformed. 50

HYDE Without conscience, without pity.

JEKYLL To a face shining with the light of new life.

HYDE Your face, the face of your true self.

JEKYLL	The face of evil, the face of the beast.

(HYDE turns from JEKYLL.)

HYDE A beast of your making, Henry. Born in you, nurtured by you. Each man and woman has their own beast, and I am yours, and you have set me free.

JEKYLL Yes, I have. And I'm glad of it.

HYDE Of course you are. Now I shall live for you, do all those things you have longed to do and never dared. You shall taste the forbidden fruit, and find that it is sweet. The sweetness of sin, the ecstasy of evil. You shall know it all! And without remorse. For the upright Henry Jekyll shall remain blameless. All shall be laid at the feet of Edward Hyde.

JEKYLL Hyde?

HYDE Your other name. Your secret name. Edward Hyde. Oh,

taste the forbidden fruit *In the Bible, Adam and Eve eat 'forbidden fruit' – an apple that God has told them not to eat. Forbidden fruit symbolises experiences or knowledge that one should not have.*

what larks we shall have! What larks and japes! I'm eager to begin. Go, now. Sleep the sleep of the innocent. Your work's finished. Mine is just beginning. I shall go out, into the world, and I shall claim it as my own.

(JEKYLL turns and goes offstage. HYDE remains, standing central. THE DAMNED of the city enter. They form a semi-circle around HYDE, and speak to the audience.)

RESURRECTION MAN   There's something wicked out on the streets . . .   90

RESURRECTION WOMAN   A beast on the loose, and it's hunting for meat.

LINK BOY   Hunting the weak, hunting the poor . . .

CRONE   Hungry for everything, hungry for more.

BEDLAMITE   The human face with a human grin . . .

HARLOT   And his eyes full of fire and a skull full of sin.

RESURRECTION MAN   It's the shadow-man from your darkest dreams . . .

RESURRECTION WOMAN   Who drinks your soul and eats your screams . . .

LINK BOY   The twist of the blade, the turn of the screw . . .

CRONE   He'll take your heart and bite it through . . .

BEDLAMITE   And nail your skin upon the wall . . .   100

HARLOT   He wants it now, and he wants it all.

(The CRONE approaches HYDE.)

CRONE   A good time you're looking for, are you, dearie?

(HYDE turns to her.)

HYDE   Yes. A good time.

larks and japes *Fun and games.*

CRONE	I thought so. *(She turns to the HARLOT.)* You, come here! *(The HARLOT approaches her.)* Go with the gentleman. *(The HARLOT hesitates.)* What's the matter with you? Go on! He don't bite. And even if he does, you'll put up with it. *(She pushes the HARLOT towards HYDE.)* You'll be pleased with her, sir. She's fresh. Fresh as a daisy. Fresh as a peach.
HYDE	How much?
CRONE	Well, now, sir, seeing as it's your first time, I'll do it for you cut-price. No cash. Just give me some of mother's ruin.
HYDE	Gin.
CRONE	That's it, sir. A nice bottle of gin. If you happen to have one on you. *(HYDE takes a bottle out of his pocket and hands it to the CRONE. She unscrews the top, takes a swig.)* And very nice it is too, sir. *(To the HARLOT.)* Go on, then. And see you treat the gentleman nice. Treat him very nice. You know what they say. A little of what you fancy does you good!

(She laughs. HYDE leads the HARLOT off. The CRONE turns to the others onstage.)

(Continues.) As for the rest of you, get out of it!

(The others go off, leaving the CRONE alone. She goes into a corner, and sits, drinking from the bottle of gin. She remains there throughout the following scene.)

WRITING In some films or plays of the Jekyll and Hyde story, Jekyll drinks the potion and physically transforms into Hyde. Here, the author portrays Hyde as a separate, independent character but still makes it clear that Jekyll and Hyde are two sides of the same person. Can you write a different version of this transformation scene, handling the transformation in a different way?

ARTWORK/WRITING Imagine you are staging this scene for the theatre. Choose one particularly dramatic moment from the scene and describe or make a sketch of what you would like it to look like onstage. Think carefully about the positioning of characters onstage, and what lighting effects you may wish to use.

SCENE 18

Sir Danvers Carew's house

LADY CAREW enters, followed by KINCH. They are talking as they enter.

LADY CAREW	Sir Danvers can only spare you a few minutes, I'm afraid. He is an extremely busy man.
KINCH	I'm most grateful that he can spare even a few minutes of his valuable time.
LADY CAREW	His time *is* valuable. Not only are there his considerable ministerial duties to attend to, but he is also engaged on the launching of a new initiative for the welfare and well-being of the entire country.
KINCH	A new initiative?
LADY CAREW	Perhaps it would be more proper to call it a crusade. And Sir Danvers Carew is at the very forefront of that crusade.
KINCH	And what, if I may ask, is the purpose of this crusade?
LADY CAREW	To regenerate the moral standing of the nation. I'm sure it cannot have escaped your attention that we are living in an age where all standards of decency and right behaviour have, sadly, gone into a most serious decline.
KINCH	Indeed.

initiative *An action or enterprise.*

crusade *The Crusades were Holy wars fought by Christians against Moslems. The term is used to mean fighting for a good cause.*

regenerate the moral standing *Improve the morals.*

LADY CAREW	Indeed, Mr Kinch. Everywhere one looks there is evidence of it. And not only among the poor and ignorant, but also among those favoured by good breeding and education – those who should know better. It is high time that someone of authority spoke out and took a stand.	20
KINCH	And Sir Danvers Carew is that man?	
LADY CAREW	He is. It is my husband's aim to bring about a renewal of those moral values and beliefs which have been the pride and strength of our nation. And will be again.	
KINCH	*(Quotes)* 'And we shall build Jerusalem in England's green and pleasant land.'	30
LADY CAREW	I hope you're not mocking me, Mr Kinch.	
KINCH	Not at all, Lady Carew.	
LADY CAREW	I, too, am engaged in the enterprise. I am, in fact, in the process of drawing up a subscription in order to bring aid to the plight of fallen women. I am modern in my outlook. I do not blame the women themselves for their condition, but those depraved men who prey upon them. With the money I raise from my subscription I intend to build a home where such women can find refuge, and thus be brought back into the fold of the righteous.	40
KINCH	That is indeed most charitable of you, Lady Carew.	

And we shall build Jerusalem . . . *A quote from the poem and hymn 'Jerusalem'.*

drawing up a subscription *Organising a collection of money; in the nineteenth century, religious or wealthy people often organised charitable funds to help the needy.*

the plight of fallen women *The unfortunate situation of prostitutes.*

depraved *Without morals.*

LADY CAREW	Then I can include your name on my list of subscribers?
KINCH	Er . . . yes . . . of course. In fact, allow me to give you something now. *(Gives her some money.)* I'm afraid it's not much . . .
LADY CAREW	It is enough, Mr Kinch. You have made your contribution, and it is not all men who can make that claim.
	(CAREW enters.)
CAREW	Now, what's all this about?
	(LADY CAREW turns to him.)
LADY CAREW	Sir Danvers, this is the gentleman . . .
CAREW	Yes, I can see that. What does he want? I don't have much time.
LADY CAREW	Perhaps you should ask him yourself. I too have duties to attend to. *(She speaks to KINCH.)* Excuse me, Mr Kinch. It's been most gratifying to meet you.
KINCH	Likewise, Lady Carew.
LADY CAREW	And I do thank you for your contribution.
	(She nods to CAREW, and goes.)
CAREW	What was all that about? What contribution?
KINCH	To your good wife's fund – for fallen women.
CAREW	Oh. That. Yes. Well – Kinch, is it?
KINCH	Yes, Sir Danvers.
CAREW	What do you want with me, Mr Kinch? Your note said it was a matter of some importance.
KINCH	Sergeant Kinch – if you wouldn't mind, sir.
CAREW	Sergeant? You're a policeman?

KINCH	Was, Sir Danvers. Alas, no more. I work now in a private capacity. Though I have taken the liberty of retaining my former title – and, yes, the matter I've come to see you about is of some importance – and delicacy.
CAREW	Is it, now? Well, get on with it, then. Don't beat about the bush. I have little time to spare. I'm . . .
KINCH	. . . A busy man. And I intend to take up as a little of your time as is necessary. I have been employed to make certain enquiries on behalf of my client . . .
CAREW	And who's that? Your client.
KINCH	My apologies, Sir Danvers, but I am unable to tell you that. My client wishes to remain anonymous, for reasons that I fully respect.
CAREW	Very well. What about these enquiries of yours? What have they to do with me?
KINCH	My enquiries – my investigations, if you like, are of a private nature. And they concern a certain person with whom I believe you may be acquainted.
CAREW	Really? And are you able to tell me this certain person's name?
KINCH	I am. His name is Hyde. *(CAREW visibly starts.)* *(Continues.)* Edward Hyde. Am I correct in thinking you have heard of him? *(CAREW turns on KINCH with sudden fury.)*

80

90

---

 anonymous *Not revealing his/her name.*

CAREW   How dare you mention that man's name in this house! How dare you come here, into my home, and speak that name to me!

KINCH   *(Rather taken aback by this outburst.)* Forgive me, Sir Danvers . . .

CAREW   I certainly won't forgive you! It's an affront . . . an insult to me . . . to speak that name – a crime.

KINCH   I take it you are acquainted with him, then?

CAREW   You can take what you like! Do you realise who you're speaking to? You know the position I hold?

KINCH   I know you are a man of some importance.

CAREW   I'll have you know I am a man of influence and high standing – and yet you dare to come here and insinuate . . .

KINCH   Insinuate what, Sir Danvers? I'm not aware that I've insinuated anything. I've simply asked you if you are associated with Edward Hyde. I did not foresee that his name would have such an unnerving effect on you.

CAREW   Damn your impudence! I know your game. Of course you'll say nothing outright. Too clever for that, aren't you? He's instructed you well, your client. Yes, I know now who he is! And I know what it is he's sent you for!

KINCH   You seem to know more than I do.

CAREW   I know this! You'll get nothing from me! Nothing! I've told him, and now I'm telling you! Not a penny! Do you understand! Sir Danvers Carew is not a man to be

affront *Insult.*

insinuate *To subtly suggest.*

blackmailed! Let him tell what he knows! It will be his word against mine, and I know who will be believed!

KINCH   I believe there's been a misunderstanding . . .

CAREW   You're damn well right there has! Your client has misunderstood me! And you can further tell him this! If he approaches me once more with his demands – or sends a lackey like you to do it for him – I shall hound   130 him from whatever hole he hides in. I shall bring him out into the light; I shall bring the full weight of the law down upon his head and crush him! Now, get out! And don't come back!

(KINCH gives a short bow to CAREW, turns, and goes off. CAREW stares after KINCH.)

lackey *Humble servant.*

DISCUSSION AND WRITING Look again at Scene 9, in which Sir Danvers Carew first appears, and compare this with the description Lady Carew gives of him at the start of Scene 18. In small groups, discuss what this tells you about Sir Danvers Carew.
● What kind of person is he?
● Do you think his wife knows what he's really like?

Use your ideas to write a character profile of Sir Danvers Carew.

SCENE 19

A backstreet, at night

CAREW turns and speaks to the audience.

CAREW
Something had to be done. It was enough to have had that monster Hyde make his demands when we met in the house of that whore; but to send someone to my home – to dare that! I knew I must act swiftly. But to whom could I turn for assistance? Who would hear and not judge? Who knew the law, and how to use it? There was only one man – my lawyer, Utterson. I decided then and there to entrust my difficulty to him. And, to this end, I wrote him a note, requesting that I meet with him at his chambers the next morning. And, not wishing to entrust a servant with this note, I went out that very evening to deliver it to his house myself.

(CAREW turns his back to the audience.)

CRONE
And he was never seen alive in this world again – except by me – and one other. For on that night, a shadow followed him through the streets. A shadow sliding silent along behind him. And he never knowed it was there. He never knowed it was death a-stalking him. For he was too high and mighty. He had wealth and title and power. He had the whole country at his command, he did, and nothing could touch him nor take him. But death has no favourites. When he calls,

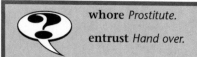

whore *Prostitute.*

entrust *Hand over.*

even kings must follow. Death strikes where he will, and he struck that night, and he struck hard and he struck with vengeance and wrath!

(HYDE enters, carrying a heavy walking stick.)

HYDE   Carew!

(CAREW turns with a start to face him.)

CAREW   Where are you going, Sir Danvers Carew? Where are   30
you bound this dark and unwholesome night?

CAREW   You!

HYDE   What business is it that draws the great Sir Danvers
Carew out of his house into the city streets? He sends
no servant, but goes himself. He takes no carriage, but
walks on foot. A secret business, it must be. A delicate
business. A business not to be spoken of in broad
daylight.

CAREW   It's no business of yours . . .

HYDE   But I think it is. Your business is my business, Sir   40
Danvers Carew. I have made it my business, as you
well know.

CAREW   Out of my way.

(He attempts to push past him, but HYDE stops him, gripping his shoulder.)

HYDE   And this letter he has in his hand. What is it? A
confession of his moral guilt? A record of his lusts and
debaucheries? Has remorse struck his soul, and is he
going to make a clean breast of all his sins? Pin them

vengeance and wrath *Punishment for wrongdoing and anger.*

lusts and debaucheries *Sexual urges and excessive sexual practices.*

to make a clean breast *To openly admit.*

to the door of the church, and cry aloud for all to hear, 'Heed me! For I have sinned and I am a sinner!'

(He snatches the letter.)

CAREW   How dare you!

HYDE   *(Looks at the letter.)* No, I thought not. He wishes to meet with the lawyer, Utterson. It is a matter of great importance. Criminal charges may be brought against 'a vile personage.' What 'vile personage', Sir Danvers Carew? Who is this 'vile personage'? And what charges are they that 'may be brought against him'?

CAREW   Listen, Hyde . . .

HYDE   No. You listen, Carew! Your law cannot touch me. I am beyond the reach of the law. In a moment I can disappear, be gone where the law can never find me. But I shall find you. There is no hole deep enough or dark enough or wretched enough where you can hide that I shall not sniff you out.

CAREW   What do you want?

HYDE   I've told you what I want. When we last met – at your 'sacred shrine' – I made it plain then what I want! And in exchange for that, you shall have – my silence.

CAREW	And I made it plain to you then, I will not be blackmailed!
HYDE	You cannot prevent it. You will pay now, or be damned for it!
CAREW	I care nothing for your threats!
HYDE	Give me what I ask, Carew. Give me the money.
CAREW	You can't harm me!
HYDE	Give me the blasted money!
CAREW	I am Sir Danvers Carew!
HYDE	And I am Edward Hyde, and I'll send you to Hell!

90

(He raises the stick. Both freeze. The CRONE speaks.)

CRONE I was there in the corner of the alley and I seen it. I seen him raise his stick. I seen him lift it in the air, and it flashed in the moonlight like the sword of wrath, and then with all his might he brought it down!

(HYDE brings the stick down on CAREW's head. The killing of CAREW proceeds now in slow motion, as the CRONE narrates.)

100

(Continues.) And again the stick was raised and again it was brought down and he fell to his knees. And though he cried out for mercy, there was none to hear. And again he struck, a terrible blow, for I heard the bone crack, and again he cried, in terror and pain. And once more and again, blow after blow, till the skull split wide and the body fell forward and cried no more, but even then Hyde did not cease. In rage and in

sword of wrath *The Crone is referring to the Christian idea, which appears in the Bible, that, at the last judgement, God's wrath (anger) will 'cut down' sinners.*

fury he did strike at the lifeless corpse, until at last all   1
rage was spent, and he let the stick fall from his hands,
and lifted his head as like a dog to bay at the moon.
And I saw his face lit and there was a look upon it
terrible to behold. A look of joy, as if some great work
had been accomplished.

*(HYDE drops the letter and walking stick, takes hold of
CAREW's body and begins to drag it offstage, as the
CRONE continues narrating. During this, UTTERSON and
KINCH enter and join the CRONE, who says to them.)*

Then he took hold of the body and dragged it off into   1
the dark. And where it is now I can't say. But the stick
he left behind, and the letter. And after he'd gone I
went and picked them up . . . *(She picks up the letter.)*
. . . And seeing the letter was addressed to you, Mr
Utterson, and having learned from others where it was
you lived, I brought it here, and here it is.

*(She hands the letter to UTTERSON, who takes it and reads
through it. HYDE has now gone off with CAREW's body.)*

DRAMA Hyde says to Carew 'When we last met – at your "sacred
shrine" – I made it plain then what I want!' In twos, devise and
perform this scene, in which Hyde tries to blackmail Carew by
demanding money in exchange for not telling Lady Carew about Mary.
You could also work in threes, and include Mary in this scene.

SCENE 20

A backstreet, at night

UTTERSON	You saw all this happen?	1
CRONE	I did, sir.	
UTTERSON	When?	
CRONE	No more than two hours ago.	
UTTERSON	And you did nothing to prevent it?	
CRONE	What could I do, sir? I'm an old woman. I was in fear of my poor old life, I was. Such rage, such murderous fury – I know Hyde, and I know he would have murdered me too.	
KINCH	You know him?	10
CRONE	Our paths have had occasion to cross. Everybody crosses my path sooner or later. And knowing what I do of him, it's the truth when I say he's no ordinary man. A demon more like is what he is. And tonight he was a demon possessed.	
UTTERSON	*(Indicates the walking stick.)* That is the . . . murder weapon?	
CRONE	Yes, sir, it is. I brought it as proof of what took place.	
UTTERSON	Let me see it. *(She gives the stick to him.)* It's covered in blood.	20
CRONE	There was a lot of blood, sir. I never seen a man bleed so much. I doubt if he had a drop left in him.	
KINCH	Why haven't you been to the police?	
CRONE	The police? I won't be having to do with them! What would the police do if I told them what I'd seen? Arrest	

	me for an accomplice, they would. Besides, it's not the first crime I've been witness to, nor won't be the last. And the best course I've found to be took is a blind eye and a dumb tongue.
KINCH	Yet you came to tell Mr Utterson of this crime.
CRONE	I did, sir. Because this was a crime of so savage a nature, that I knowed I couldn't keep it locked away, so to speak, and would have to tell someone. And there being that letter, addressed to the gentleman, and him therefore being involved . . .
KINCH	Involved?
CRONE	The murdered man was on his way to see Mr Utterson . . . I seen it as my duty to tell him . . .
KINCH	Your duty?
CRONE	Yes.
KINCH	You had no thought of reward?
CRONE	Reward, sir? Why no, sir, no. Bless you, I never thought of no reward. And yet . . . if the gentleman . . . if Mr Utterson was to see fit . . . to offer by way of gratitude . . . some token . . .
KINCH	You wouldn't refuse.
CRONE	That would be ungracious of me. If he was to make the offer . . .
UTTERSON	Which he will. *(Takes out some money.)*
CRONE	Thanking you kindly, sir. You are most . . .
UTTERSON	This payment absolves you of all further interest in

 accomplice *Somebody who assists a criminal in carrying out a crime.*

	this case. The knowledge of it you have handed over to me. Whatever is to be done about it from now on, I shall do. Do you understand?

KINCH A blind eye and a dumb tongue.

CRONE I have your meaning, sirs. Yes, I have it very well. *(She takes the money.)* Blind and dumb I shall be. The world shall know nothing of this from me. Thanking you both, kind sirs. You are gentlemen, for sure. Thanking you both most kindly and gracious.   60

(She turns and goes off.)

UTTERSON Poor Carew. How he must have suffered. He was not . . . the best of men, I know. But, even so, to die like that . . . I thought I knew something of the world . . . but I didn't know until now it was filled with such horror.

KINCH There is horror in the world, Mr Utterson. It arises in many places, and it assumes many forms. And, at present, horror has arisen among us, and it has assumed the form of Edward Hyde.   70

UTTERSON How long do you think it will be before this crime is known to the police?

KINCH Certainly Carew's disappearance will be reported as soon as his wife discovers it – which will be most likely within the hour. After that, it depends how long it takes for the body to be discovered – which in turn depends on what Hyde has done with it. Unless, of course, you go to the police yourself.

UTTERSON I intend to! This monster must be apprehended and

---

absolves *Removes blame.*

assumes many forms *Takes on many forms.*

brought to justice! But there is also Dr Jekyll to be considered. From what you've discovered in your enquiries, and from what I've discovered myself just now, his association with Hyde is even closer and deeper than I'd feared. I believe him to be in mortal peril.

KINCH   You will go and see him, then?

UTTERSON   Yes. Before anything else. As he is my friend, I owe it to him.

KINCH   If I might remind you, Mr Utterson, you tried to reason with Dr Jekyll before . . . when he showed you the will . . .

UTTERSON   This time he will listen! I'll make sure of it.

KINCH   Before you go, sir, if I might ask you one thing. You said just now that you yourself had discovered something. What was it?

UTTERSON   (Holds up the stick.) This. The murder weapon. The thing with which Hyde beat poor Carew to death. I've seen it before, many times. It belongs to Henry Jekyll.

---

apprehended *Caught, arrested.*

in mortal peril *In danger of his life.*

SCENE 21

Jekyll's house

Immediately, JEKYLL enters and approaches UTTERSON, speaking as he walks on. KINCH moves to the side of the stage and watches the scene.

JEKYLL	Let me see that stick!	1
	(UTTERSON gives the stick to JEKYLL, who stares at it in horror, then continues)	
	Yes! Yes, it is mine. I can't deny it! Oh, God, what have I done?	10
UTTERSON	I trust you haven't done anything . . .	
JEKYLL	No, of course not –	
UTTERSON	How did he come by it?	
JEKYLL	He has . . . many things of mine . . . All he has, I have given him.	
UTTERSON	Henry. Listen to me. I don't ask what your associations are with this man – or why you have taken him under your care . . .	20
JEKYLL	You'd do best not to. If I were to tell you, you wouldn't believe what I said.	

UTTERSON	But I implore you as your friend to break off that association now, and have nothing more to do with him!
JEKYLL	Yes, of course. You're right. You're absolutely right. I must – I will. I've made a terrible mistake, but I'll put it right. I will have nothing more to do with him!
UTTERSON	It's a relief to hear you say it.
JEKYLL	But I want you to make a promise to me.
UTTERSON	What's that?
JEKYLL	Don't go to the police.
UTTERSON	What?
JEKYLL	Don't tell them what you know about this . . . unfortunate affair.
UTTERSON	Unfortunate affair! Is that what you call it? There's been a murder committed! A most brutal murder!
JEKYLL	I know.
UTTERSON	And the perpetrator must be brought to justice!
JEKYLL	No! No, he mustn't! Think what would happen to me if he was. He wouldn't hesitate to implicate me in his crimes – even though I've had nothing to do with them – I'd be ruined – my whole life . . .
UTTERSON	You're asking that he goes free?
JEKYLL	Yes.
UTTERSON	Free to commit other crimes.

implore *Beg.*

perpetrator *Person responsible.*

implicate *Connect with a crime.*

JEKYLL	He won't! I promise you.
UTTERSON	How can you be sure?
JEKYLL	I am sure! You must trust me. I . . . know him. And I promise you faithfully that, from this day forth, you'll hear nothing more of Edward Hyde. Nothing. It will be as if he's vanished from the face of the earth.

50

(JEKYLL turns from UTTERSON and moves a few steps away, as KINCH walks back towards UTTERSON.)

KINCH	And do you believe what he said?
UTTERSON	*He* believed it, I'm sure of that.
KINCH	So you intend to honour his request?
UTTERSON	For the time being. I'm willing to give him the benefit of the doubt. We'll wait and see if he makes good his promise.

60

KINCH	And if he does not?
UTTERSON	Then in all conscience I shall have to go to the police. But until then, let us say that the case is closed.
KINCH	Then I presume that my services, as they say, are no longer required.
UTTERSON	On the contrary, Sergeant Kinch. They are very much required. Keep watch for Hyde, look for any hint or sign of his continued presence. If he is still here, hunt him out. But let us both pray to God that you fail, and that this whole, dreadful business is truly at an end.

70

(UTTERSON goes off.)

honour his request *Respect his wishes.*

KINCH   (*Addressing the audience.*) So I kept watch. I listened for the merest whisper of Hyde. But I never heard of the man again. It was as if he had truly vanished from the face of the earth. And not only him. For, from the time Utterson last spoke with Jekyll, the doctor too was never seen again. The two of them, disappeared clean out of the world. As if where one went, the other must also go, the two of them bound fast together, irrevocably and eternally. And yet the story, I know, isn't over. For the presence I felt that night, when I walked alone in the dark streets, I feel it still, in all places, a great shadow cast upon the world, touching us all in the darkest places of our hearts. And it fills me with foreboding and fear, and I live in dread of the human form it may one day acquire.

(*KINCH moves to the side of the stage, and remains there.*)

irrevocably and eternally *Hyde and Jekyll are connected forever and cannot be separated.*

HOT-SEATING In small groups, one of you takes on the role of Utterson, and the others question him. Try to find out:
  a why he believed Jekyll when he told him the affair was over
  b whether he found his friend, Jekyll, changed in any way
  c what his thoughts are on the whole affair.

DISCUSSION As a class, read through Kinch's speech at the end of the scene, then discuss what you think the writer is saying in this speech, especially with the closing lines: '. . . I feel it still, in all places, a great shadow cast upon the world, touching us all in the darkest places of our hearts. And it fills me with foreboding and fear, and I live in dread of the human form it may one day acquire.'

SCENE 22

The street where Jekyll lives

JEKYLL turns and speaks to the audience.

JEKYLL   An end. An end to horror. What began as a dream of   1
            freedom became a nightmare of tyranny. Myself slave
            to myself, my own base and twisted nature. Unbidden
            now, he came, the creature I gave birth to, a monster
            feeding on my own flesh. What demons dwell within
            us! What devils inhabit the black pits of our being!
            And shall we acknowledge them? Claim these things of
            darkness as our own? No. Banish them rather from all
            knowledge! Leave them to the darkness, let them twist
            and writhe in torment, let them fade and wither at last   10
            to nothing. Only then shall we be free.

            (HYDE enters.)

HYDE   Free?

JEKYLL   Yes. Free of you. It's taken courage, and strength, but I
            have done it. From this moment on, I shall never again
            have to suffer the face of Edward Hyde.

HYDE   What makes you so certain of that?

JEKYLL   I've disposed of that which called you forth. The

Myself slave to myself, my own base and twisted nature. *Jekyll means that he is in the power of Hyde, who represents the bad side of his personality.*

unbidden *Without being summoned/called; Jekyll means that Hyde appears without Jekyll having taken the potion.*

And shall we acknowledge them? . . . *Taken from a speech about a monster in Shakespeare's play* The Tempest.

	powders I created, I've destroyed. You are back in your cage where you belong. I consign you once more to the darkness, and there in the darkness may you rot!
HYDE	You shall rot, Henry Jekyll! Not me! Did you believe it was that ridiculous concoction that brought me forth? You think I am to be summoned and dismissed like a servant? I came because I chose to come; I am here because I choose to be here; and I shall not go until I choose to go – and that will never be.
JEKYLL	That's not so – it can't be – you're my creation . . .
HYDE	No. You are *my* creation. Before you were, I was. And after you are gone, I shall be. I was always the strongest part of you, and each day I grow stronger. For now I have tasted blood, and my power is become mighty!
	(The CRONE enters.)
CRONE	Just give me some of mother's ruin!
HYDE	You hear them? The voices of the dark.
	(The LINK BOY enters.)
LINK BOY	Light your way, sir?
HYDE	They're calling me, calling me to them.
	(The RESURRECTION MAN enters.)
RESURRECTION MAN	A little of what you fancy does you good.
HYDE	Calling to the dark from the dark.
	(The HARLOT enters.)

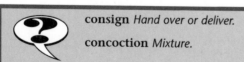

consign *Hand over or deliver.*

concoction *Mixture.*

HARLOT	Looking for a good time, are you, dearie?
HYDE	Out there, that is where true life lies.
	(The RESURRECTION WOMAN enters.)
RESURRECTION WOMAN	Where's the money? Just give me the blasted money!
HYDE	The life of the senses, the life of the flesh.
	(The BEDLAMITE enters.)
BEDLAMITE	Hold him down! Keep him still while I finish the job!
HYDE	The one life I was meant to live.
	(THE DAMNED of the city now stand onstage in a semi-circle, with HYDE centre stage. JEKYLL cries out)
JEKYLL	No! You shall not! You shall not live!
	(Although HYDE speaks to JEKYLL, he does not look at him, but remains facing outward.)
HYDE	But I do live. It is you, my poor, weak friend, who do not. You who cannot live any longer.
JEKYLL	What do you mean?
HYDE	You share your life with me. Two lives inhabiting one body. But that cannot continue. Flesh and bone and blood cannot bear it. One of us must prevail. The stronger must prevail – the survival of the fittest. And I, you must admit, am the stronger, and most fit.
JEKYLL	No . . .

50

60

One of us must prevail *One of us must win/be successful.*

the survival of the fittest *This was the controversial theory of the scientist Charles Darwin, published in 1859, that animals and plants have adapted over time; Darwin believed that humans were descended from apes.*

HYDE   As my strength waxes, yours wanes. You were only ever half alive. You and all your kind. Compared to me, you are nothing, and soon, you shall be nothing, and I shall be all.

JEKYLL   It can't be!

HYDE   But it is. Look at me, my friend. The face you see is your true face. I am your one and only self. And I am the last thing you will ever see.

JEKYLL   God forgive me. God help me!

HYDE   God doesn't hear you. You're cursed and cast out. Gone to the devil. Go to him. He waits for you. As he waits for me to walk his ways in the world.

(THE DAMNED of the city turn to JEKYLL and move towards him, gradually closing in around him. As they do, they murmur, softly and threateningly, their voices dark with menace.)

 As my strength waxes, yours wanes *As my strength increases, yours decreases; Hyde is getting stronger as Jekyll weakens.*

THE DAMNED
Look into the night,
Look into the dark.
Look into the night,
Look into the dark.

(Soon, JEKYLL is completely surrounded by them. Their voices grow louder as they raise their arms, take hold of him, and slowly push him down until he can no longer be seen. As he disappears among them their voices rise even louder.) **100**

THE DAMNED
Look into the night,
Look into the dark.
Look into the night,
Look into the dark.

(Then, their voices stop, abruptly, and there is silence.)

HYDE
For I am eternal. I am that which lives forever in man. And now I am free and I shall stride forth across the earth, and all shall know my name. **110**

(THE DAMNED of the city turn and, separately and in silence, leave the stage. JEKYLL is no longer there, and HYDE stands alone.)

(Continues) And such larks we shall have. Such jolly larks and japes.

(He turns, and walks out through the central door, closing it firmly behind him. KINCH steps forward and speaks to the audience.)

KINCH
Let us speak only of facts. Let this mystery remain unsolved. Let the door to which it leads remain unopened. For I would not enter there. **120**

(He goes off.)

I am eternal *I will go on forever.*

WRITING In Scene 21, Kinch stated that Jekyll and Hyde were 'never seen again'. Re-read this scene carefully, then write what you think happened to Jekyll 'in reality', and explain why you think he disappeared.

ARTWORK Imagine you are directing this scene onstage. Make a sketch of how you would want the stage to look during one of the key dramatic moments in the scene. Think carefully about where characters will be positioned onstage, and what lighting effects you may wish to use.

DISCUSSION Kinch's final lines are the last lines in the play, they are very important. Read them through again, then, as a class, discuss what you think is meant by these lines. Why should the mystery remain unsolved? Why should Kinch not wish to enter the door that leads to it? What do you think the writer is trying to say in these lines?

LOOKING BACK AT THE PLAY

1   WRITING: STYLE OF SCENE
There are two kinds of scene in this play. One kind is what we might call
'realistic'. These are the scenes that follow Kinch's investigation and
gathering of evidence, and include most of the flashback scenes. The other
kind is 'non-naturalistic'. These are the scenes which attempt to dramatise
what's going on inside Jekyll's mind, and usually involve him, Hyde and the
Damned of the city. Go through the play and divide the scenes into these
two kinds. You could set them out in a table like this:

Non-Naturalistic	Naturalistic
Scene 1	Scene 2
Scene 6	Scene 3
etc.	etc.

2   DISCUSSION: STYLE OF SCENES
As a class, discuss why you think the dramatist chose to make some scenes
non-naturalistic. What do you think he was trying to achieve by doing this?
Do you think the story itself could have been dramatised in an entirely
realistic way?

3   ARTWORK: FILM POSTER
There have been several films based on this story. Imagine you are designing
a poster for a new film. The image on the poster is taken from a scene, or
number of scenes, from the film. Decide what scene or scenes you think best
sum up what the story is about, and design the poster. The poster should, of
course, contain the title, and also maybe a phrase or two designed to
encourage people to go and see the film.

4   DISCUSSION: WHAT THE PLAY IS ABOUT
On one level, the play is a mystery horror story. But, on another level, it's
also saying something about human nature. As a class, discuss what you

think the play is saying about human nature. Do you agree with the view put forward in the play? Do you think the play says anything that is relevant to modern society? Try to support your ideas with examples from the text.

5   **DISCUSSION AND WRITING: STAGING A SCENE**

The play is meant to work as a mystery and horror story. In small groups, discuss which scenes, or parts of scenes, you think could be tense or frightening onstage. Then discuss what you would do if you were directing that scene to make it as frightening as possible. When you've done this, make notes on the scene you've chosen, why you chose it, and how you would stage it.

6   **DRAMA: A MISSING SCENE**

One scene that doesn't appear in the play but could have been included after Scene 14 might have been as follows:

> Mr Lanyon is talking to Kinch again. His character seems much altered from when we saw him last. His calm detachment is gone, he is agitated, highly nervous. He tells Kinch of a meeting he has had recently with Jekyll. As Lanyon narrates, Jekyll enters for a flashback scene of Lanyon's story. Lanyon turns from Kinch to enact the scene with Jekyll. Jekyll tells Lanyon he has come at last to prove to him that the theories he held years ago were not wild. Lanyon is perplexed by his old friend's sudden reappearance, especially in the light of what Kinch told him about being in some kind of trouble. But his perplexity changes to horror as, before his eyes, Jekyll transforms into Hyde. It is the monster Hyde who now mocks and sneers at Lanyon, threatening him, finally leaving him, the broken wreck of a man. At this point, the flashback scene ends, and Lanyon turns back to Kinch. He's weeping, starting to rave. The warder from the previous asylum scene enters with a strait-jacket, and we realise that Lanyon is in the madhouse. Lanyon tries to escape from the warder, and the warder and Kinch chase and finally capture him, in a deliberate echo of the earlier scene. Lanyon is dragged off raving about 'the foul fiend'. Kinch does not know what to think.

In small groups, devise and act out this scene. There will need to be at least five characters – Kinch, Mr Lanyon, Dr Jekyll, Mr Hyde, and the Warder – and maybe a sixth, if you decide to bring Utterson in at the end of the scene, and have Kinch relate to him what's just happened.

Plan the scene carefully, then improvise and rehearse it several times, before performing it to the rest of the class.

7   WRITING: MONOLOGUES
A monologue is a piece of writing in which a single character speaks his or her thoughts and feelings about a particular incident, or tells the story of something in which he or she was involved. Writing a monologue is a good way of beginning to understand a character. Choose one of these characters to write a monologue for:

1 Richard Enfield: telling the story either of the night he came across Hyde, or the night Jekyll first arrived at Mary's
2 Mary: Her meetings with both Jekyll and Hyde
3 Utterson: His thoughts on the whole case, after Jekyll has disappeared
4 Lady Carew: After she's been informed that her husband has been found murdered
5 Kinch: His views on the whole case
6 The Crone: How she met Hyde, and the story of the murder.

Before writing a monologue for your chosen character, research that character by looking at every scene in which they appear; reading carefully what they say, how they say it, how they behave, what they think and looking at what others say and think about them. Then, when you think you have a pretty good idea how that character feels, thinks, and speaks, begin to write your monologue.

Remember, it's important in a monologue for the character to speak about their thoughts and feelings, as well as simply relating a story.

8   ARTWORK: DESIGNING A PROGRAMME
Design a programme for a theatre production of the play. Choose any actors to cast in the roles. Give the programme an eye-catching title page and include a cast list, the time, date and place of performance, and a brief explanation of what the play is about.

9   WRITING: A NEWSPAPER ARTICLE
Sir Danvers Carew's body has been discovered. Because he is a renowned and important politician, the story is front-page news. You're a journalist who has been investigating the story behind the murder, and have interviewed several people, including Lady Carew, Carew's servants, the police, and others. Write an article about the murder, including the information you've managed to discover from interviews and investigations.

10 **READING AND DISCUSSION: PLAYSCRIPTS**

Below is an extract from Stevenson's story, on which Scene 4 of the play is based. The character who is speaking is Richard Enfield.

'I was coming home from some place at the end of the world, about three o'clock of a black winter morning, and my way lay through a part of town where there was literally nothing to be seen but lamps. Street after street, and all the folks asleep – street after street, all lighted up as if for a procession, and all as empty as a church – till at last I got into that state of mind when a man listens and listens and begins to long for the sight of a policeman. All at once, I saw two figures: one a little man who was stumping along eastward at a good walk, and the other a girl of maybe eight or ten who was running as hard as she was able down a cross-street. Well, sir, the two ran into one another naturally enough at the corner; and then came the horrible part of the thing; for the man trampled calmly over the child's body and left her screaming on the ground. It sounds nothing to hear, but it was hellish to see. It wasn't like a man; it was like some damned Juggernaut. I gave a view halloa, took to my heels, collared my gentleman, and brought him back to where there was already quite a group about the screaming child. He was perfectly cool and made no resistance, but gave me one look, so ugly that it brought out the sweat on me like running. The people who had turned out were the girl's own family; and pretty soon the doctor, for whom she had been sent, put in his appearance. Well, the child was not much the worse, more frightened, according to the Sawbones; and there you might have supposed would be an end to it. But there was one curious circumstance. I had taken a loathing to my gentleman at first sight. So had the child's family, which was only natural. But the doctor's case was what struck me. He was the usual cut-and-dry apothecary, of no particular age and colour, with a strong Edinburgh accent, and about as emotional as a bagpipe. Well, sir, he was like the rest of us; every time he looked at my prisoner, I saw that Sawbones turned sick and white with the desire to kill him. I knew what was in his mind, just as he knew what was in mine; and killing being out of the question, we did the next best. We told the man we could and would make such a scandal out of this, as should make his name stink from one end of London to the other. If he had any friends or any credit, we undertook that he should lose them. And all the time, as we were pitching it in red hot, we were keeping the women off him as best we could, for they were as wild as harpies. I never saw a circle of such hateful faces; and there was the man in the middle, with a kind of black, sneering coolness – frightened, too, I could see that – but carrying it off, sir, really like Satan.'

Compare this passage with Scene 4, and, as a class, discuss the difference, and why you think the writer chose to make the changes he did in writing the scene.

11 **RESEARCH: BIOGRAPHY**

Robert Louis Stevenson was born in Edinburgh in 1850. He was often ill as a child, and, in his early twenties, he developed a severe respiratory illness. It was then that he decided to become a professional writer. To help ease his condition, he spent much time travelling abroad, and eventually he settled on the island of Samoa, where he became known as 'The Story Teller'. He died there of a brain haemorrhage in 1894.

See what more you can find out about Robert Louis Stevenson and the times he lived in.

12 **FINDING OUT: THE FIRST 'DR JEKYLL AND MR HYDE'**

One night towards the end of 1885, Robert Louis Stevenson had a nightmare, and woke to tell his wife, Fanny, that he had dreamed 'a fine bogey tale'. He immediately sat down to write it, and had finished a first draft of the Jekyll and Hyde story within a few weeks. He gave it, as he did all his works, to his wife to read. When she had finished it, she told him that he must certainly not publish the work in its present form, and insisted that he re-write it. We don't know what it was she objected to, because Stevenson burned the work and re-wrote it. It was this second version that was published and which made Stevenson's name as a writer. But what was it in the first version that Fanny objected to so strongly? Was it perhaps too explicit in its detailing of Jekyll's 'vices', did it deal too openly and frankly with the 'dark' side of Victorian middle-class life? We can only guess.

Try to find out more about the circumstances surrounding the writing of *The Strange Case of Dr Jekyll and Mr Hyde,* and see if you can unravel some of the mystery.

NEW DRAMASCRIPTS

Already one of the most popular collections of plays available, the **Dramascripts** series includes contemporary dramas and adaptations of classic pre-20th century texts. **New Dramascripts** are the result of extensive research with English teachers. The series now offers more demanding literature and a broad range of enjoyable new adaptations. The complete list of **New Dramascripts** published in 1998/99 is given here:

Available now:

A CHRISTMAS CAROL	0-17-432547-9
BILLY LIAR	0-17-432549-5
THE DIARY OF ANNE FRANK	0-17-432550-9
OLIVER TWIST	0-17-432548-7
THE HOUND OF THE BASKERVILLES	0-17-432557-6
SILAS MARNER	0-17-432552-5
THE TERRIBLE FATE OF HUMPTY DUMPTY	0-17-432554-1
UNMAN, WITTERING AND ZIGO	0-17-432555-X
TREASURE ISLAND	0-17-432560-6
HOMER'S ODYSSEY	0-17-432562-2
THE SPECKLED BAND	0-17-432561-4
PRIDE AND PREJUDICE	0-17-432558-4
DICING WITH DEATH	0-17-432596-7
THE MOONSTONE	0-17-432553-3

Available May 1999

THE WOMAN IN WHITE	0-17-432595-9
WUTHERING HEIGHTS	0-17-432559-2
JANE EYRE	0-17-432597-5
DR JEKYLL AND MR HYDE	0-17-432599-1
THE ISLAND OF DR MOREAU	0-17-432600-9
THREE CLASSIC THRILLERS	0-17-432598-3

These titles are available individually or in money-saving group packs.

Enquiries	Fax
01264 342992	**01264 342788**
Direct ordering	Email
01264 342995/6	**nelinfo@nelson.co.uk**